Help Your Child with a Foreign Language

Opal Dunn

Berlitz Publishing Company, Inc.
Princeton   Mexico City   Dublin   Eschborn   Singapore

To my husband and children
from whom I have learned much

Copyright ©1994   Opal Dunn
Copyright ©1998 BPCI

Published by Berlitz Publishing Company, Inc.
400 Alexander Park, Princeton, NJ 08540-6306, USA

First published in the United Kingdom by Hodder & Stoughton Ltd.

Berlitz Trademark Reg. US Patent Office
and other countries -- Marca Registrada

All rights reserved. No part of this book may be reproduced or
transmitted in any form or by any means, electronic or mechanical,
including photocopying, recording or by any information storage and
retrieval system, without permission from the Publisher.

Printed in Singapore
1 3 5 7 9 10 8 6 4 2

ISBN 2-8315-6806-4

Contents

Dear Parents,

Help Your Child with a Foreign Language will create hours of fun and productive learning for you and your child. Children love to learn with adults, and working together is a natural way for your child to develop second-language skills in an enjoyable and entertaining way.

In 1878, Professor Maximilian Berlitz had a revolutionary idea about making language learning accessible and fun. These same principles are still successfully at work today. Now, more than a century later, people all over the world recognize and appreciate his innovative approach. Berlitz Kids™ products combine the time-honored traditions of Professor Berlitz with current research to create superior products that truly help children learn foreign languages.

Berlitz Kids™ materials let your child gain access to a second language in a positive way. The content of this book is based on the experience of an internationally known author and teacher of foreign languages. What's more, the projects and activities in the book will delight your child, since they stimulate and sustain interest. In addition to the activities, you may want to consult the Useful Phrases section (towards the back of the book), and use it as quick reference.

We hope that *Help Your Child with a Foreign Language* will provide you and your child with an enjoyable learning experience.

The Editors at Berlitz Kids™

Introduction

Help your child with a foreign language. You may wonder if you can do it. Remember, you have already taught a language: you helped your child from zero to fluency with his first language. Re-using and developing some of these same techniques, supported by materials and careful planning, you can help your child again. Part of the secret to successful foreign-language learning for a child is knowing that he is making progress that is recognized and appreciated by his parents.

What I have written is based on my experience as a teacher trainer, materials writer, consultant on bilingual education and, more important, as a parent. I was determined to bring up my own children tri-lingual, in spite of the fact that I had no formal qualification in a foreign language beyond school—only interest and enthusiasm.

I hope what I have written will enable you to make the quality of help you give to your child, or the children you work with, more effective. It can be used as a basis for beginning any foreign language, even English, if it is not your family's own language.

You may find the first three chapters hard reading. It is important to read them, as they'll help you understand how learning takes place and how you have already helped in language learning. Often after lectures people come up to me and say, "Now I understand what was going on and my role in it. A pity I didn't before."

HELP YOUR CHILD WITH A FOREIGN LANGUAGE

All the examples are taken from English—it was simpler to use English as the base and let you transfer it to the foreign language you and your child are working in. I've also included a lot of useful phrases in some of the major world languages to give you an idea of how you and your child can use a foreign language straightaway. In a book of this size, it was not possible to include more languages or languages with a different script.

You may already be using many of the suggestions, or have used them without realizing it when you helped your own child learn to speak his own language. Some may be quite new. Please remember, however, that they are only suggestions. You may need to adapt them to match your child's as well as your family's style.

To be fair to your sons and daughters, I have used *he* and *she* in alternate chapters.

Have fun and don't underestimate your child. Most young children enjoy learning a foreign language and do it amazingly well, if you can get the way of learning right for them and can see things through their eyes as well as your own.

Opal Dunn

CHAPTER ONE

Can a parent help?

<u>"What learning situations can I, as a parent, help in?"</u>

This book aims to help parents of children in the following situations:

- beginning at home;
- attending a foreign-language club or camp;
- learning a foreign language as a subject at school;
- attending a bilingual school;
- living abroad;
- going abroad for vacations;
- having a foreign-language speaker in the home—a binational family, an au pair, or a student;
- foreign friends or neighbors.

Foreign languages interest children

"I can count in three languages," boasted five-year-old Jane in the playground. "Oh, I can count in four languages," Tom added. "Listen. One, two, three. Un, deux, trois, that's French. Uno, dos, tres, that's Spanish, and ein, zwei, drei, that's German." Neither of them was learning a foreign language at school.

Young children are interested in foreign languages. They are proud to show off the little they know about them. They can recognize their different sounds and they enjoy telling you about them. Some children even notice how people from foreign countries speak. They'll comment on how they use their mouths and lips differently.

"My French teacher talks like this," Dan, aged four, said as he mimed how his French teacher spoke with her lips close together in a long narrow shape. He had noticed that French speakers tend not to open their lips as wide as English speakers.

Learning a foreign language is part of a child's holistic development

Many children find learning another language fun. They feel it's something they know how to do and take it in their stride. More than two-thirds of the world's children speak two or three languages. Their families expect it of them. Since the opportunities exist within their home or society, it's accepted as quite normal. To be able to use two or more languages is not something that the child thinks of as being separate from other things he is doing. A foreign language is just one of the many things he's busy finding out about and learning: it's part of his holistic development.

The number of young children learning foreign languages before the age of 10 or 11 is increasing. The advantages of being bilingual or trilingual are gradually being recognized and appreciated by schools and families. The steady growth of transnational communication and business, as well as the increase in global travel, will result in more staff being expected to work in more than one language and one culture. Advertisements for bilingual staff, rare in the late 1980s, are today common and likely to multiply.

Is learning a foreign language difficult?

Ideas that it might be difficult or too demanding for children are largely in the minds of adults. Such ideas may reflect the adults' personal difficulties. Possibly as children they encountered problems at school due to poor teaching methods and the lack of good materials and other learning opportunities. Maybe they didn't have much support or encouragement from their parents and learning a foreign language wasn't thought of as something important in their home.

Children are quick to pick up attitudes—good and bad. Self-fulfilling prophecies work both ways. His mother's comment that "I was good at German at school" rings in a child's ears on his first success. He feels that he's already on the same successful path, and if that's the way he feels, he'll most likely succeed. Alas, the converse can happen at the first failure. "My Dad wasn't any good at Spanish, and I'm the same." Before he's gotten anywhere, he's given up. The self-fulfilling prophecy has taken over.

Children soon mirror attitudes—good and bad—so be careful not to let anyone pass on their negative attitudes. They leave lasting impressions, especially in the early stages of learning, and may stick for life.

Modern language learning opportunities

Times have changed a lot since our grandparents learned a foreign language at school—if they did.

- Expectations in the family, in society, and the world are different.

- More is known about how children learn their own and foreign languages.
- Many new opportunities and types of material exist today for listening to and using foreign languages. These make learning an easier and a more real activity for learners.
- Opportunities exist to hear and see foreign languages being used within your own home and society—for example, in newspapers, and on radio and television.
- Foreign travel enables learners to get first-hand experience of the foreign language and culture.

Personal relationships—the keystone of language learning

Young children learn best where the personal relations between the child and the teacher are close, warm, and encouraging. Many of us enjoy something today, or are good at it, because of our relationship with the teacher of that subject.

Learning language relies even more than other learning on a close personal relationship. You can practice the piano or paint by yourself, but for language to develop you need someone with whom you can interact and make conversation. If there is no dialogue, you can't learn how to speak (see page 21).

Adults can make conversation as and when a situation calls for it. In a normal situation if someone talks to them, they will have no difficulty in replying and even entering into a discussion. Children, however, can't turn language on in the same way if they don't know the adult. Children can't manage to talk and communicate with someone if they don't feel at ease with them. For interaction to take place, there has to be a personal relationship between the child and the adult.

As each child is an individual and reacts differently, it is important for the adult to know the child well. Without being close to a child and knowing how he learns and communicates, an adult finds it difficult to understand his intentions and respond to his day-to-day growing needs. The adult who spends the most time with the child is usually the parent.

The parent as a language teacher

Your child learned to speak at home. You taught him. Even if he went to pre-school, most of the language learning took place at home. At pre-school he was one of a crowd, and there was little time for individual one-to-one chats with the teachers. Most talk through which language was learned usually took place at home with you.

You can help your child learn a foreign language in much the same way. You can give him the same individual attention and encouragement. You can provide him with good learning opportunities. Even if you can't speak a foreign language well yourself, you can manage, since many types of materials exist to support your spoken language (see page 155). And speaking the language well is only one ingredient in the recipe for successful learning. You can easily provide all the other ingredients. You did it before when you taught your child to speak.

For a child, learning to speak a foreign language is not very different from learning to speak his own language. His ability to use language increases as he uses more language in conversation. Through your caring relationship and sharing of well-planned opportunities, your child will begin to talk to you. He will absorb a foreign language in much the same way as he learned his own language, but at a quicker speed. Without a close bond between adult and child, learning to speak a foreign language is not as successful.

It is arguable that the parent is the child's best, first foreign-language teacher. It is understandable that, once past the beginning stages, a parent may want to look for other learning experiences and expertise. This does not mean that the parent's role is over. Interest and support in what the child is doing is still important for motivation.

Why the parent?

- The parent knows his own child better than a teacher does.
- The parent knows through experience and intuition how to judge his child's temperament and moods.
- The parent is more sensitive to his own child's individual:
  — needs and interests;
  — level and way of speaking his own language;
  — ability to do things;
  — ways of learning.
- The parent knows how to gain and maintain his own child's interest.
- The parent generally has time for more one-to-one sessions than a teacher in a classroom situation.
- The parent can plan follow-up and continuity more accurately and on a day-to-day basis.
- The parent can organize language-learning activities to match the child and to fit into the daily or weekly routine.
- The parent is often a more patient listener.
- The parent can influence the child's attitudes toward cultures and people. The family's other attitudes may be different from those of the school or classmates.

Is a child happy learning from the parent?

- A child is used to learning from his parents and does so without being conscious that he is actually learning.
- A child feels secure learning with his parent at home.
- A child knows that the family is interested in what he is doing and wants him to succeed. This gives him confidence and helps him to cope when, as sometimes happens, schoolmates make fun of foreign-language learning.

- Learning can be tailored to fit the child's needs. He can learn when he most feels like it.
- Learning together may give a child an added opportunity to confirm his parents' love, and to appreciate their interest, encouragement, and praise.

Goals for the parent?

- Make sure language learning is fun for both of you.
- Stimulate an interest in a foreign language and culture.
- Provide the child with the type of language he needs and can use.
- Find out ways to continue learning beyond the home and school.

Possible achievements and benefits for the child

Short term

As a result of sharing, your child should:

- increase his ability to concentrate;
- learn from you how to study and find out information;
- gain self-confidence;
- be more positive towards learning.

Long term

Through your efforts and continued support, your child may:

- develop a life-long interest and enjoyment in learning and using foreign languages;
- develop positive and sensitive attitudes toward foreign cultures and peoples;

- understand more about language and how it communicates needs, ideas, etc.;
- understand and be able to use his own language better;
- increase his general knowledge;
- enhance his self-esteem.

Questions parents ask

"Will it interfere with my child's schooling?"

Results show that the child who works in two languages is, in the long run, at an advantage because:

- he sees his own language differently through learning another grammar;
- he improves his own learning skills;
- he learns how to learn;
- he adds a new dimension to his interests;
- he becomes more flexible and tolerant in his outlook;
- he is more creative in his ideas and ways of solving problems.

"Can I help even if I can't speak the foreign language well?"

Language content is only part of the package needed for learning a foreign language. Shortcomings in your spoken language can be compensated for by use of some of the better audiovisual materials available.

For success, **your child** also needs your:

- regular time;
- patience;
- encouragement and praise.

For success, **you** need to understand:

- the role you played in helping your child learn his own language;
- how children learn a foreign language.

Children learn by imitation. The first accent they hear spoken in a foreign language will be their first model. However, children are flexible and capable of altering their pronunciation to match the different models they hear. They are in fact capable of speaking several dialects in their own language (see page 29). They can do the same in a foreign language. Don't underestimate them and don't judge them by adult standards.

Final thoughts

The crucial influence of parents on their child's achievements is now widely accepted. It is well known that talkative families produce children who can communicate well using a rich vocabulary. By helping your child with a foreign language, not only will you expand his scope for life, you will find that you also bring a new dimension into your family. Foreign-language experiences will be shared by you all, even if it is only talking about and tasting new food. Foreign-language expressions, jokes, and songs may become part of your in-family conversation. This may remind you of how you shared in-family expressions and experiences when your child was learning his own language.

CHAPTER TWO

Learning your own language: how parents helped

For a child, learning a foreign language is not radically different from learning her own language. In fact, a large part of the task is the same, as similar processes are involved in both. For this reason it is vital to understand how your child went about learning her own language and how you helped her. Perhaps you haven't realized that without you, she wouldn't have learned to talk so easily.

You may not have realized when you were looking after your young child that you were also helping her to learn to talk. Actually, you were closely involved in her learning processes. By providing her with things to do and discussing with her what she was doing, you helped her.

When you took her to feed the birds in the park, remember how you talked to her as you got the bread ready. Once you got there, you explained to her where to throw the bread and she excitedly repeated your words and phrases. What you were doing unconsciously played an important part in both your child's language and mental development, as learning language is linked to learning about things.

Children learn by doing. They learn language by taking an active part in something that interests them and is right for their age and ability. Adults call it playing, but to the child, play is a serious worklike activity. In the child's mind no division exists between work and play until she learns the idea from adults or older children.

Think back to how your child busily did things and chatted about them with you when she was four years old. First your child made sense of what was going on, and then she worked out the language that went with it. She was interested in what she was doing, and you extended her knowledge and language by talking with her about it.

> *"Can't open it," she said, trying to turn the top on a plastic bottle.*
> *"Turn it this way," her father said, miming how to turn it.*
> *"Can't. Won't turn."*
> *"Look, try again. Turn it away from you. Like this." Her father*
> *mimed how to turn it.*
> *"Done it."*

You talked to her in ways that made it easier for her to understand. At the same time you increased her use of language. During this process, she absorbed some or all of the new language.

Often it was difficult to stop her playing. She was totally immersed in the situation and was concentrating hard on what she was doing. There was no direct teaching of language. You didn't stop her to talk about grammar rules. You didn't tell her that this is a verb and that is a noun. She was discovering the rules for herself through using language.

Why learning depends on your collaboration

Nearly every conversation with a child provides her with an opportunity to learn how to talk as well as how to learn through talk.

It is through talk that the parent explains the way that she sees the world. It is through talk that the child discovers more about the world.

> *"Bus," says the 18-month-old girl.*
> *"A bus," her mother confirms.*
> *"Bus," the child reflects.*
> *"Yes. A big bus," her mother says.*
> *"Big bus," the child echoes.*

In this little dialogue the child has learned about language—about the article *a* (although she didn't pick it up and use it at this stage), and the adjective *big*, and that it comes before the word *bus*. She has also learned that her mother sees the bus as big—not little. She has learned about size. She had already heard the word *big*, but hadn't used it before.

A lot of what young children know has been learned from conversations in which they have taken part. Absorbing both information and language depends on interaction between the child and the adult. It's rather like throwing a ball back and forth between two people. The language passes from one to another in conversation. As it does, the child and parent negotiate what is meant. To get the meaning clear to each other, they may have to pass the ball back and forth several times.

Sometimes the child may throw the ball first to initiate a conversation, and sometimes the parent. Most parents seek opportunities to start off conversations with their young children. They tend to use more questions than when talking to adults but don't use questions such as "Is it big?" which only call for a *yes* or *no* answer. They know these sorts of questions don't lead on to further conversation.

> *"All gone," said two-and-a-half-year-old Ted.*
> *"Yes. Your biscuit's gone," his mother replied. "You've finished it."*
> *"Car all gone."*
> *"Yes. The car's gone. Dad's gone to work."*
> *"Dad gone," Ted continued.*

"Yes. Dad's gone in the car."
"Bye, bye, Dad."

In this conversation the mother confirms and develops what the child says and, in doing so, unconsciously helps in learning. The child shows his innate ability to transfer language and make the little language he knows go a long way—a skill that persists into adult life. Have you ever tried stretching the few ready-made phrases you know in a foreign language to help out in the hotel, the store, or on the train when you're abroad?

The degree of collaboration and the quality of the conversation make a huge difference to the child's rate of language development. Many parents, especially mothers, know intuitively how to talk to children in the special way that facilitates language learning. These language skills are often referred to as "parentese." If you've forgotten about how you used parentese, try sitting next to a young parent and child on the bus or join the same supermarket checkout line. You'll be able to recognize many of the skills.

What are parentese language skills?

Apart from the natural empathy between parent and child and the desire to help their child progress, parents know their child best. They act as their child's continuity. Parents are sensitive to their child's needs, and their antennae are sharpened to their child's desire to communicate. They pick up the slightest cue that others may miss. This, together with their intimate knowledge of their child's achievement level and interests, helps parents in interpreting what their child is trying to say.

Talk usually starts from where the child is and builds on from there. The parent often reflects back to the child what she wants to know. In this way the child can confirm that she was right and can then re-use the language in a more sophisticated way. Even if the child starts with only one word, a parent intuitively knows at what level to pitch the reply. Using parentese language, the parent gradually builds up a conversation.

> *"Green," says the two-year-old twin as he pushes a toy stroller.*
> *"Yes. This one's green, isn't it?" his mother adds.*
> *"Blue," he continues, referring to the blue stroller pushed by his twin brother.*
> *"Yes. That's right. His is blue."*
> *"Blue, green."*
> *"Yes. We've got two strollers, a blue one and a green one," his mother continues.*

Most parents use parentese without knowing it. They'll talk to their child or any young child and use it and then turn to the adult standing next to them and talk like an adult. Parents rarely make a mistake and use the wrong level.

Through using parentese, parents intuitively encourage their child to acquire more complex language and vocabulary. They extend the meaning, which stimulates the child to think and communicate further ideas. Parents manage to squeeze language out of their child. Other adults can't do the same unless they too use parentese skills.

How parents talk using parentese

- Parents automatically slow down their rate of speech and pronounce words more distinctly, but without distorting the way they say the words or altering the rhythm of what they say. Compare this with the way many older people alter their speech to talk to speakers of other languages who don't understand. Some just shout, which isn't very helpful, others isolate each word in an artificial way.
- They may emphasize a difficult word by accompanying it with a gesture and other forms of body language.

- They tend to use a softer, more affectionate, higher-pitched voice. It is thought that it is easier to listen to a higher-pitched voice.
- They often pause at the end of a sentence to give their child an opportunity to echo a reply.
- They may stop more often to check that their child has listened and understood before they continue. They know there is no point in going on unless she has understood.
- They use real language. They may include their child's own words or special in-family words, but don't use continuous baby talk or pigeon English.
- In speaking they naturally and often unconsciously:
  — repeat language;
  — reword the same message:
    "Where's your sock?" says a father to his four-year-old son.
    "Don't know."
    "Can you see your sock?" his father says, rewording the message. "Where's your sock?"
    "No."
    "Oh look. There's your sock. Over there. On the chair."

The boy's father introduces an alternative structure to express the same meaning and then follows it by repeating the original question;
  — expand language:
    "Bag."
    "Mother's bag. Yes, that's mother's bag. Mother's big bag," her mother adds.*
    "Big bag," her two-year-old daughter replies.
  — simplify complex language. By doing this they bring it down to the child's level. Parents do this when they tell the story of a picture book instead of reading the long and difficult printed text;
  — use shorter and less complex sentences that focus on what is familiar to the child;

GIBSONS AND DISTRICT
PUBLIC LIBRARY

— use their voice in special ways: they alter the pitch or speed to add suspense or awe; they emphasize part of a phrase to hold interest; they use tone and facial gesture to signal that the child should repeat;
— use body language more than when talking to adults. They use their arms and hands to demonstrate a point. They often place their face nearer to the child and may even exaggerate their mouth movements to help understanding. Communication through eye contact is normal and expected by many children;
— use concrete examples and real things to help understanding.

Why interaction is vital for language learning

Interaction provides a child with:

- an experience in which language is used and learned;
- a content that can be learned.

Look back to the interaction between the twin and his mother on page 24. Not only did he learn language, he learned that they had two strollers, one blue and one green. Through interaction in conversation that employs parentese language techniques, learning takes place naturally. At his own pace the child builds up to fluency.

The degree of fluency depends greatly on the quality of the interaction. When one of the interactors only hears but doesn't listen properly, the quality of the response may not provide the child with an opportunity for learning. A mere acknowledgment — such as *mm* or a single word such as *yes* or *no*—doesn't provide any reason for the interaction to develop any further.

There is an important difference between hearing and listening. Hearing involves receiving and understanding sounds.

Listening is more concerned with paying attention and getting meaning from something that can be heard. In fact, listening involves making a conscious effort. For good interaction to take place, the listener has to record accurately what is said. Some people are known to be better listeners than others. Parents get used to paying attention to their children and being good listeners. Communication with children depends on attentive listening to language as well as searching for nonspoken information and combining both with parental intuition. Eye contact between the parent and the child is an important part of listening and understanding.

Where children have little opportunity for interaction or the quality is poor, language development is not as rapid or as good. For example, some parents who left their children's daily care to au pairs or maids who spoke only very basic English were puzzled to find that after about a year their children's language ability had hardly increased. The reason was quite simple. The adults looking after them didn't know how to use parentese techniques in English and so couldn't help these children develop their own language.

Parents continue using parentese techniques even when their children seem to talk quite well. Depending on the age of their child, or even the mood, they adjust the amount and type of parentese they use to match their child's immediate needs.

Parentese language skills are innate to adults. Most adults use them automatically, irrespective of the language, when talking to any young child. Teachers who are good with young children use them in a modified form called "teacherese."

How language develops

There are three stages of development:

Stage 1	The **silent period**
Stage 2	The **intermediate period**
Stage 3	**Breakthrough**

The second and third stages overlap until children become fluent speakers.

The silent period

Communication takes place between a baby and adults from birth. Initially the child's communication is nonverbal. Remember how your baby communicated to you that she needed feeding? During this silent, or nonverbal, period of development, children are silently mapping the language they hear onto their own world. At the same time they are busy working out the basic language categories. They continually update, adjusting to the new information they acquire. This adjustment continues throughout a child's life until her language skills match those of her adult world. Children instinctively know how to learn language. It is as if they have an innately guided program which is preset to go through the same processes, irrespective of the language.

Children progress at their own speed. They cannot be hurried out of the silent period. When they have built up an adequate bank of categories and systems and worked out how to use them to create language, suddenly, from one day to the next, they begin to talk.

A silent period can be extended artificially by parents or siblings who anticipate a baby's needs and answer every question for her.

> **Mother:** *"Where's your teddy bear?"*
> **Sister:** *"It's on the kitchen table."*
> **Younger sister:** *"I'll get it. Wait there, Tom."*
> So Tom, aged three, waits, saying nothing until Teddy is pushed into his arms. He smiles but doesn't say any form of thanks.

In situations such as this, the young child is never given any reason to communicate. He is supplied with all the information he needs. There is no information gap essential for communication to take place. He expresses his desires and feelings through body language. Every opportunity to get into conversation is blocked by his family, who answer for him before he has a chance. Similar blocking can occur with older children when parents eagerly answer every question visitors ask their children.

The intermediate period

The joy and pride that parents show when their baby babbles her first string of lip-made sounds resembling words such as *papa* or *mama* is infectious. Remember the enthusiastic way you told your extended family and friends that your child had begun to talk? This show of enthusiasm is important to the child as it motivates her to go on trying to talk. It makes her realize that talking is a way of making her parents happy and pleased with her. This is something she wants to do.

As children's language develops from using one word to two, parents notice that children begin to:

- compress sentences into two meaningful words:
  "The dog is in the garden" is compressed to "dog garden."
  The child has put together the two key words and possibly the only ones she understands in what she hears her parent say. She has left out 'the,' 'is,' 'in,' and 'the,' which are not vital for understanding.
- to leave out word endings:
  "The dog's barking" is reduced to "dog bark."
  Most parents know how to decipher what their child really means. What's happening here and now, together with clues from gesture and the way words are stressed, provides additional help.
- ask questions. They may begin with question words:
  "Where ball?" "What that?"
  or by ending on a higher questioning note:
  "Me go?" "Cat chair?"
  Children continue for a long time to make ordinary statements into questions by ending them on a higher note:
  "You're going outside?" is used instead of "Are you going outside?"

This type of inter-language is common at this stage of development. Parents are used to it and reply by repeating back the full version of what the child said. The child then may repeat the full version again before the conversation continues. In this way the child gets practice in hearing and using language.

Children are quick to pick up blocks of ready-made language, often called prefabricated phrases. They imitate them perfectly, without having any idea about how many words they contain or about the grammar:

> *Stop it.   Don't want to go.   Don't know.   Bath time.*

As their language ability develops they begin to use partially prefabricated phrases: they incorporate language about something they are presently doing into part of a phrase they already know:

> *"**Give me** the scissors" becomes "**Give me** the paste" or*
> *"**Give me** the glue."*

Breakthrough

By the age of three, most children are beginning to create their own language. They're stringing proper sentences of three or four words together. They're capable of quite sophisticated conversations. No longer are words such as *in* and *on*, or the articles *the* and *a* omitted.

The ability to speak develops in a predictable manner. The same preset schedule appears to be followed irrespective of the child's cultural background. Created language begins to dominate over prefabricated. Inter-language mistakes become less frequent.

By age six, it is thought that a child already understands around 4,000 words, although she cannot necessarily use them herself. She can speak complete sentences using a great deal of grammar correctly, including past and future verb tenses. By six, most children also understand what writing represents, and many will already be reading. This means that many understand the differences between spoken and written language.

By age six or seven, many children can communicate using more than one form of their own language. For many, this means being able to communicate in the language used at home as well as the language used in the playground, if the two are different. Children who can communicate in two types of language generally know when and where it is appropriate to use each language form. They rarely make the mistake of addressing grandparents in their playground language. They know it won't be appreciated! Surprisingly, some parents aren't aware that their children can also speak the local playground language fluently. They find out by chance when they arrive unannounced at the playground. Often they can hardly believe their ears!

By seven or eight, it is difficult to find many differences between the way parents and their children talk. Of course their child's vocabulary won't be as large and the topics of conversation obviously won't be the same, but the structures used in speaking will be similar. So will the speech sounds. As children get older, how often are they mistaken for their parent by people at the other end of a telephone?

How does understanding develop?

Children's understanding develops very fast. But, like adults, they understand more words than they can say.

By 18 months, children begin to understand instructions. Remember when you dressed your child you said, "Put your arm in here," or in a different tone of voice said, "Don't do that." She began to understand simple instructions because they were connected to doing things and were part of the daily routine. Probably what you said was accompanied by body-language clues. As you said, "Say bye bye to Dad," you waved, indicating what she should do.

As time went on she learned to make meaning by selecting the key words in what you said and guessing the rest. This ability to understand by gist, in other words making sense by filling in the gaps between the words you know, is an important step in all language learning.

Most parents naturally structure what they say in a way that helps children to develop gist understanding. The following example shows how over several weeks the parent adjusted the language and content of her instructions to fit her child's developing ability to understand.

Stage 1 "Put it there." *(giving her the book and then pointing to the table)*

Stage 2 "Put your book there." *(pointing to the table)*

Stage 3 "Put your book on the table."

Stage 4 "Put your book on the table and go into the kitchen."

This parent helped her child to understand by sequencing what she said. As her child understood more of the language, she used fewer body-language cues. Most likely her child only understood key words such as *put, book, table,* and *kitchen.* Children appear to have an ability to sift out the language that is important to them.

Parents intuitively sense when what they have said is beyond their child's understanding. When they've noticed that this has happened, they'll say the same thing again but using language that their child already knows. In this way they'll help her to recognize that both mean the same thing.

The importance of motivation

Motivation is essential for any learning, including learning language. Praise and encouragement help to motivate. They are recognition of success or potential success for doing things and not for the use of spoken language. It's accepted that learning your own language is something that is innately programmed. The child has her own inner drive, and learning how to speak will take place at her own pace and with help from parents.

Children, especially as they get older, need to be motivated if they are to go on and do new things. It's while doing new things that they use language in interaction; if they aren't motivated to do them, their language skills won't increase, and without them they can't learn to their full potential.

Children are quick to sense their parents' feelings and to know when and how to please them and attract praise. **Praise** is not the same as **encouragement**, but both serve to motivate. Praise is generally given for something completed successfully: "Well done," "That's nice," "I like that," "That's very good." Encouragement is given while the child is doing something. It is intended to assist successful achievement: "Try again and I think you'll get it this time," "Just a bit more and then it's finished." Both are important, but praise should not be routine. Wise parents know when it's justified and so do children. If children get used to regular praise, they can be very discouraged if you forget to give it. This can demotivate.

Although praise and encouragement are not often given to help children improve spoken-language skills in their own language, they are regularly used to motivate them when they are learning a foreign language.

Optimum learning times

Each child is individual and each learns differently. From recent research it appears that girls learn and use language more easily than boys.

Most young children have an inner drive to explore and find out. They have periods when they seem to be more eager and capable of learning than others. During these intense learning periods, they concentrate and stretch themselves to capacity. These sensitive periods can last hours or days, depending on the child. Once over, all becomes normal again. Although tired by her efforts, she is obviously satisfied by her achievement.

A five-year-old girl decided she wanted to learn how to write. She desperately wanted to write like her brother, who was two years older. For five days she practiced writing letters of the alphabet in every free moment, pestering adults to explain how letters were made or to check that she was making them correctly. By the fifth evening she was copying from her brother's reading book. A smile of satisfaction spread across her face when her father said, "Well done. That's beautiful writing. But that's Ric's reading book." "Yes. I know," she replied. She'd achieved what she wanted. Now she could rest and unwind.

Learning only takes place when a child is concentrating. A young child's attention span is short but flexible. It depends on mood and the quality of the interaction as well as the match between the activity and the child's interest and ability. Children soon lose interest if something is too difficult for them or they can't understand.

Parents know when their child is really concentrating. Eye contact is one of the ways of holding attention. Parents know that once a child's eyes begin to wander, her concentration is waning. How often have you tried to get concentration back once it has been lost? With very young children you might as well give up and change the activity once concentration has gone.

Mistakes

Until children start to read, they have little idea about words. They mostly don't know how many words there might be in what they say. They hear a flow of sounds that are broken into groups rather than words.

When asked to write down *What are you doing?* a six-year-old boy wrote:
Wotcha do   ing?

He thought he heard three words, so wrote it like that.

Language is governed by systems that make it understandable. Children have the ability to analyze the language they hear and work out the systems that govern it. Adults call these systems grammar. Between the ages of three and four, children are noticeably puzzling out the systems of English. This is shown by the mistakes they make from time to time when they over-generalize a rule. So a four-year-old girl might say:

"Where did my Mummy goed?"	(verb *went*)
"What did you took?"	(verb *take*)
"They've comed."	(verb *come*)
"Two mens."	(*a man*, plural *men*)
"Her very better."	(*much better*)

What she is doing is logical. She is applying a regularity to an exception. Using *goed, mens, took,* and *comed* shows that she was working out systems herself and wasn't just copying what her parents said.

Children assume that adults will understand what they say. Parents are used to this, and to them what is said—the intended meaning—is generally more important than how it is said. They don't scold or correct their child, saying, "You've made a mistake," or "That's wrong." If they did, they might inhibit her. They don't even bother to stop the flow of conversation: they merely reword what their child said as part of it. By the next time she uses the word, she has corrected it.

Correction by adults has little value. What the child works out for herself she remembers. What an adult tells her she generally forgets. Where a mistake persists, there is still no gain in overtly correcting. The child will adjust it to the adult model at her own speed.

The four-year-old girl continued to say, "Where goed my mommy?" for seven months. No correction was made, as the girl was continually correcting her own mistakes, adjusting her language to match her parents'. Her father continued to reply to her question by repeating the question in the correct form and then replying.

> *"Where did your mommy go? She went to the market with Aunty Bunny."*

These forms are a normal phase in a child's language development. It's unfortunate that adults refer to them as mistakes.

Playing with language

Children love to play with language. Through playing with language they find out more about the sounds and systems that make it up.

They like stringing together rhyming words, real or made-up ones:

Real words   **Made-up words**
bat hat sat cat mat fat   blat wat zat

or replacing initial sounds in words:

"big burger" replaced with "tig wurger" and to parents' disapproval "pig wurger."

The degree to which they can play with language is linked to their all-round ability to use language and their familiarity with rhymes, poems, and chants, as well as songs.

Questions parents ask

"Are girls better at talking than boys?"

Girls generally learn to talk earlier than boys, although by the age of three, boys seem to have caught up. As children get older, girls are as a whole better at using language than boys. Certainly, girls talk more in the classroom and with their family and friends. Most girls don't seem to be inhibited about using language. Talk seems to be more important to them, and through talk they develop their ability to use language and increase their vocabulary. Boys don't seem to need to talk like girls: often a single statement says all they want.

"Is it true that the eldest child always talks more fluently?"

It depends on many things, including the child's own personality, family life, and gender.

The first-born has a longer time with both parents to herself. This means that there is plenty of time for interaction, not only in conversation but through books. The second and third children have to share their parents' time and so get less individual attention and opportunity for one-to-one talk. The same is true in the case of twins or triplets. Only children are privileged in the same way as the oldest in a family, except that it lasts throughout childhood.

Final thoughts

Language skills can be developed. This, however, requires time, patience, and effort on the part of adults responsible for children. If families are not used to spending time talking to each other and discussing, children will not be used to seeing and hearing those around them use language for communication. Children who are brought up in families where language experience is limited are more likely to have limited language skills themselves.

Language is essential for all learning. It is generally found that the better the child's language skills are in her own language, the more capable she will be of learning and using a foreign language. Children are endowed with built-in linguistic abilities that, it is thought, are distinct from their general intelligence. That a child may be a special child with special educational needs does not mean that she won't find learning a foreign language an enjoyable, enriching, and worthwhile experience.

How do children learn a foreign language?

Many of the difficulties of learning a foreign language exist in the minds of adults. Learning a foreign language won't be difficult for your child if you can replicate some of the same conditions that proved successful when he was learning his first language with you. They include creating the same supportive atmosphere of sharing and talking about what's going on. Too many adults underestimate children's ability to pick up languages. This may be because many don't understand how children learn language, and a foreign language in particular. Some imagine that children learn a foreign language in the same way as adults, but more slowly and with the content modified and represented in childlike images. Others think that the role of the adult should be tutorial. This might work for subjects such as history and science, but it isn't how children learn language.

Learning language is something young children know how to do innately. They can do it if adults let them and don't hold them back. They've already had the successful experience of learning their own language—in fact, some of them are still doing it. They have worked out their own language learning strategies. They know how to analyze language to find out the systems that govern it. They can reuse these same strategies for learning a foreign language, and they'll enjoy doing so, if we give them enough of the right type of interesting and fun opportunities to interact with us.

To begin with, they'll want to learn spoken language as they did when learning their own language. The time they spend on spoken language will depend on how quickly they progress. Once they can say simple things, those who can already read well in their own language will quite naturally want to find out about reading and writing in the foreign language (see chapter 7).

Children's ideas about foreign language learning

In children's minds learning a foreign language is not a subject. It's not something that is learned in isolation, even though it might appear so on a school timetable or in the way adults talk about it. It includes crafts, singing, science, and math—it's cross-curricular.

Mother says, "Don't forget it's German after school today."
"What did you do in Spanish?" asks Father.

For children all language—their own or a foreign language—is embedded in learning about everyday life. It's part of their holistic development.

Children are interested in the differences between languages. From a very early age, they seem to notice when adults speak in a different language. They'll often pick up some of the different sounds of a foreign language and tell you that it sounds like this . . . muttering some of the sounds. Parents of different nationalities who use their own language in parentese are amazed how soon their baby can distinguish between the two languages.

Children are proud to show off their language skills. They are often to be found boasting about how they can speak in a foreign language.

James, aged four, told me: "I can say bottle in three lan-
guages: American, English, and French." He continued: bot-

*tle with a New York accent, bottle in British English, and
finally bouteille in French. He had lived in New York and
London and attended French classes in his kindergarten.*

How do children learn a foreign language?

The case of Japanese children who come to Britain with their family and attend an American elementary school provides a clear
example of how children learn a foreign language. The same basic
pattern with six-, seven-, and eight-year-old boys and girls has
recurred regularly over the last seven or eight years. American ele-
mentary-school teachers, many of them parents themselves,
though with no special training in teaching English as a foreign language, have said that they begin to recognize this common pattern
of foreign-language learning.

The Japanese children come to American elementary school:

- motivated to learn;
- with expectations that they can learn. They know their parents and extended family expect them to succeed. They
  have heard about or met other Japanese children who can
  speak English;
- with sufficient "survival language" to cope. This consists of
  words like *toilet, yes, no,* and a few phrases such as *My
  name is Akiko*;
- with a feeling of security, as they have some knowledge of
  what to expect. They have been at school in their own country and there are some similarities. They have already visited
  the American school and met their new teacher;
- knowing that their parents are encouraging and supporting
  them.

The first week at school is difficult—more difficult for some than others. Depending on the school and the degree of foreign-language support and encouragement from parents, most young Japanese children settle down remarkably quickly.

Silent period

Communication takes place from the moment the parent has left the child at school. Teachers of young children are skilled in using teacherese—a modified form of parentese. This helps interaction, especially in the first weeks. Although these Japanese children can say very little in English, they soon interact with the teacher and classmates through body language and especially eye contact. They know how to communicate like this. They've done it before at an earlier age when they learned their own language. These children are in fact passing through a similar silent period. They're busily taking part in school activities, copying what others do if they don't understand, and saying very little themselves. The daily routine of classroom management necessitates repetition of language, which makes understanding easier.

As these children can already communicate in their own language, their purpose and needs in learning a foreign language are not the same. Their maturity and understanding of their environment and how it works means they can speed up some of the stages in learning language. They don't have to find out about something before they learn the language that goes with it. For example, they no longer need to spend time identifying things with one word—*book, table, chair*. They've already done this in their own language and now all they need is to learn the equivalent word in the foreign language. However, to learn single words isn't satisfying, as they can't use them to begin communication. To say *table* by itself doesn't start a conversation, which is what they want to do. It's easier and more fun to learn items of vocabulary by playing a game (see page 105).

Children learning a foreign language know how to use spoken language—how to speak in phrases and sentences, ask questions and use commands. They know about the power of language and how it can make another person react. They've found out in their own language what happens if they say "Stop it. Don't want to. I'm tired." They want to be able to use a foreign language in the same way. They want to be able to say the same sort of things and get the same sort of results. If they can't say what they want, they can become frustrated or lose interest.

To speed up the process of speaking, adults can provide children with useful ready-made or prefabricated phrases. They learn these as blocks of sounds in the same way as they did when they learned their own language.

"Put it here. Stop now. Put your things away. It's playtime. Come out." If parents then transfer the same language to a variety of situations, the children hear these same phrases over and over again and soon pick them up.

Carefully selected, useful songs, chants, and rhymes—all a form of prefabricated language—help to contribute to the child's bank of language (see page 112). Using rhymes provides a shortcut to a lot of language at an early stage of learning. It gets children used to the sounds of the foreign language. It also gives them the satisfaction of feeling that they are speaking a lot of the foreign language, which they long to do as quickly as possible.

Intermediate period

After about one month most of the Japanese children moved beyond the silent period and began using prefabricated language.

Go away.   *Not yet.*   *Stop it.*   *It's mine.*

Prefabricated language was central to the development of language in these early stages. As when learning their own language, children soon began to transfer the few phrases they knew to different situations. "Not me" was used by one of the Japanese girls each time she didn't want to take part in something.

Practicing language

Most children seem to get great pleasure from being able to repeat language aloud to themselves. It's a form of practicing. They're gradually gaining control over their mouth and lips so that they can make them move the way they want. Learning to coordinate this with the right volume of voice in a foreign language is an exciting challenge. Children sometimes repeat aloud in their normal voice and sometimes in a sort of whisper, as if they are only practicing saying the sounds. Japanese parents told the teachers that they couldn't understand why their children went around the house repeating the same phrase in English over and over again. They had forgotten that their children had done the same thing when they were learning their own language.

Pronunciation

The Japanese children picked up language by imitating what they heard around them. Their pronunciation was just like the other children in the class. Often they were to be seen twisting their necks so that they could get nearer to American children's faces to see exactly how they spoke. They recognized when a sound they made didn't quite match the language they heard and went about changing it themselves. In the same way as in learning their own language, they refined sounds until eventually they matched those of the other children. None of the difficulties which Japanese adult learners have with *l* and *r* sounds, for example, were noticeable in these children's speech. In individual chats, when the teacher noticed a mistake, she never commented. Using parentese techniques, she repeated the correct form of speech hoping that the child would pick it up and correct himself. She was confident that this was the right way to cope with mistakes, as she knew the child could self-correct as he had done before when learning his own language.

Learning through language

Day by day these children were capable of taking a more active part in what was going on in the classroom. In some things they even began to excel. This was generally in subjects that depended on less language for understanding, such as art and crafts, or where the children already had learned the content in Japanese school. Concepts only have to be learned once. In mathematics the children had already learned the concepts in Japanese school, so they only needed to learn the new language labels for the numbers and signs. Once they knew these, they understood and began to get good marks. Successes like these were important, as they not only increased self-esteem and standing among classmates, but proved to the children that they could also be successful working in a foreign language. Success leads to further success and motivation.

As their ability to use language increased, so these children interacted more and more within the classroom and the school. They began to add partially prefabricated phrases to the prefabricated phrases they were already using.

> **This is** *my book.* **This is** *my bag.* **This is** *my lunch.*
> **Where's** *Tom?* **Where's** *the ball?* **Where's** *my glove?*
> **It's** *mine.* **It's** *Mary's.* **It's** *Mrs. Green's.*

They were in fact beginning to create their own language.

Breakthrough

At the end of three months of total immersion in an American school, teachers related that from one day to the next, the Japanese children began to talk. In fact, the children were so pleased with their newly acquired skill, teachers found it difficult to stop their chattering. It was as if something had happened overnight that made it possible for breakthrough the next day. Suddenly, these children found they could create their own language to talk about things within their own experience. Unconsciously they were building new language by combining bits of language they already knew. To their delight they found they could even initiate a discussion and sustain it. Although they continued to speak using prefabricated and partially prefabricated language, the amount of created language they used increased daily, to become the most important part of their speech.

This "overnight breakthrough," as teachers term it, is reminiscent of what happens when a young child breaks through to create sentences in his own language. This type of breakthrough is not unique to children learning their foreign language in American elementary schools. Teachers in British schools report similar experiences after four or five months with immigrants learning English. Non-French speakers in French schools take about the same length of time to achieve breakthrough.

The length of the prebreakthrough period depends on the amount and types of exposure to the foreign language as well as the degree of home support. Where there is no home support, learning takes longer. Where parents don't understand the foreign language, but still give support, learning is quicker, as the support motivates and creates positive attitudes. In British classrooms where programs include projects and group activities, interaction between staff and other children is more frequent. This makes learning language easier for the child.

Comparison of languages

After about five months several of the Japanese parents reported that their children began to criticize their pronunciation.

> *"You don't say it properly."*   *"That's not right."*
> *"You don't say led." (red)*

The Japanese parents were naturally disappointed. Instead they should have rejoiced. The criticism showed that their children knew enough about the sounds of English to distinguish between the sounds made by native speakers and their parents. A remarkable analytical achievement for children of the age of seven or eight.

Japanese parents also related that their children often answered the phone of American friends. These friends were amazed that it was impossible to tell who was speaking—the Japanese child or the American friend. The telephone is an excellent way of testing language skills as the listener has no clues as to the nationality of the speaker apart from the voice.

It was interesting that at this stage the children made no comments about the word order used by their parents, which was often different from that of American people.

Interpretation skills

After about seven months most of the children started to interpret for their parents when they were shopping, in a restaurant, or even talking to their teacher. They translated what was said in the foreign language and sometimes added cultural information if they felt their parents needed it. Somehow they appeared to be able to judge what their parents would not know about local culture. Switching from one language to another seemed natural. In fact, each language was accompanied by the correct body language in a way that made you feel that a child could take on two different characters.

The two languages were completely separated. Only where a word or phrase was known by the parents and didn't exist in Japanese—such as *team colors* (red teams, green team, etc.), a phrase specific to school—or the children didn't know the word in Japanese, did children mix languages. It wasn't in fact mixing, but a type of word switching that can only take place when you know a language quite well and both you and the person listening have shared the same experience.

Mixing languages

In the initial stages of learning, there may be some mixing of languages. Mixing is part of the process of getting languages sorted out. Some children rarely or never mix. Although parents worry about mixing, most normal children seem to sort out the problem themselves as they gain experience, providing adults don't hassle them. Parents need to deal with the problem in the same way as they do other mistakes: make no comment and repeat the statement correctly in one language.

The ability to speak two or three languages and not mix them is well known to parents of different nationalities who use their own language with their children.

My four-year-old daughter speaks three languages: Italian with me, French with her father, and English with her nanny. She identifies each of us with a different language and answers in each language without making a mistake.

Thinking in a foreign language

It's clear that at some stage, children begin to think in different languages. In the case of the Japanese children interpreting for their parents, they were obviously thinking in two languages. They were no longer silently translating everything back into Japanese and then thinking about it in Japanese. They hadn't the time. At what point each child began to think in both languages differed from child to child.

Children appear to pass through the same three stages in learning language, whether it's their own language or a foreign language. Knowing about these stages will help you to understand more about how your child learns and how best to support him. Although you may not be able to help your child reach breakthrough, you can help him get a long way towards it by careful planning and sharing experiences with him.

Questions parents ask

"What is a bilingual person?"

The debate about bilingualism and what is a bilingual person continues, and as situations change within countries and the world, so the discussion will develop.

From the child's point of view there appear to be two major

stages in bilingualism that should be recognized.

Stage 1

The child at this stage understands that there is not only one way of naming an object.

"What's this?" pointing to a picture of a car.
A car *in English.*
But the same thing in German is ein Auto.

This is a difficult concept for a child to grasp, and understanding it depends on a degree of maturity. Children are taught and understand a one-to-one relationship between words and things.

The mother says *spoon,* and then points to a spoon. The child matches a picture of a car to a car. The child learns that one equals one.

Now they have to understand that a car can have two names and that both are right. Neither is wrong. They are used to thinking that something is either right or wrong. Now we are telling them that neither is right or wrong—there are just different ways of labeling the same thing.

A child who has grasped this concept can be considered as an emergent bilingual.

Stage 2

When a child working in two languages can:

- create language in both to express meaning;
- think in two languages separately;

he can be considered as a bilingual.

"Is a bilingual child equally good at each language?"

A child who can speak two languages cannot necessarily use each language with the same degree of competence to talk about everything. The language the child knows will relate to the experiences which the child has had in that language. For example, if a child has played a board game in Italian, he will know all the game language in Italian. He may not be able to talk about it in English, because he doesn't know the special vocabulary in English. If he does talk about it in English, he'll substitute Italian words for the words he doesn't know in English.

Where experiences have taken place in both Italian and English, he will be able to talk about them in either language with fluency. For example, he will be able to talk about his bicycle in both languages as he rides at home and also with his Italian friends. Language ability increases with use. Where languages aren't used they become rusty.

For a child the language most used tends to be dominant. The position of dominance can change. Polish children attending an English-speaking summer camp abroad find their English becomes dominant. They complain, "Oh dear. I'm forgetting my Polish," as they have little opportunity to speak Polish. When they return to Poland for the long summer vacation, their fluency in Polish soon comes back, and as they are not using English, Polish becomes dominant again, and English moves into second position. Parents often worry about children forgetting languages. This is natural if children don't have the opportunity to use them. The remedy is to provide children with interesting and fun experiences in which they can use the language (see page 100).

Since children learn language by taking part in activities that generally involve some culture, young children learn about a foreign culture at the same time as they learn the language. Without realizing it, they become not only bilingual but bicultural (see chapter 19).

"I'm not a trained teacher, does it matter?"

- You taught your child to speak his own language, and you can help your child with the first stages in a foreign language.

- Your support, encouragement, and praise are vital for his

success.

- You can plan opportunities to match your child's interests and learning needs.
- You can see that he is surrounded by positive attitudes to learning a foreign language.
- What you don't know you can manage to find out (page 160).
- What you feel you can't do well you can supplement (page 155).

"Would it be better to begin with a native speaker?"

Getting the right pronunciation is only a small part of learning a foreign language correctly.

The other factors are:

- developing positive attitudes;
- being motivated;
- matching learning needs;
- developing language through parentese language skills.

The native speaker may not get these other factors right, as she won't know your child as well as you. She may not get her level of language right for your child, and your child may find understanding the foreign language more difficult, as it entails learning new language accompanied by new body language. The native speaker may use teaching techniques common in her country but different from the way young children learn language. She may not be used to using parentese techniques in teaching.

It may be better to introduce a native speaker only when your child has some grounding and confidence in the foreign language. In the meantime you can use recorded material to support your spoken language.

It is important not to get over-anxious about letting children hear only the standard accent in the foreign language. After all, what happens in your own language? A form of Global English, Global French, Global German, etc., is emerging, which uses a form of spoken language that can be understood worldwide. Half an hour of switching channels, especially on cable TV, is sufficient to make this development apparent.

Children need to be able to communicate—in other words, to be understood and to understand. Once they can do this, they can alter their accent to fit their needs. Parents underestimate children's ability. They're very good at it in their own language and can do the same with foreign accents, too (see page 31). The same children who played on a beach in the South of France with local children will speak French differently when they stay with a family in Brussels. But in both cases communication will take place and more language will be learned.

"Must I provide total immersion?"

In total immersion a lot of learning time is wasted, as much of the language is too advanced for the child's learning level. Although the level should always be a little in advance of the learner's if he is going to learn something new, too much in advance can be both time-wasting and discouraging.

Guided total immersion is more time efficient as it provides the child with activities that are planned to include language that is right for his present level of learning.

To guide successfully the adult needs to underpin planning with a hidden language syllabus of language items that the child needs for communication (see page 63). These items differ in some cases from what the adult beginner needs. In guided total immersion the child is exposed to targeted language activities. In this way the child's task of sifting through language to find what's useful to him at his stage of learning is greatly reduced.

Using a hidden syllabus for reference ensures that children are getting the language they need for communication. Children are creatures of the present. They like to do things instantly, and this includes talking in a foreign language. If, after a period of learning, they still can't say in a simple form what they want or feel, they can become frustrated.

"Will my child go through a silent period?"

All children go through a silent period during which they build up their own bank of knowledge about the foreign language and work out the systems. They need time to do this.

It is possible to cut short this stage by using rhymes, chants, and songs (see page 112). As in learning your own language, the contribution to all-round learning made by rhymes, etc. should not be underestimated.

"What do I do if my child makes a mistake?"

First you must decide what sort of mistake it is. Mistakes can be thought of in three general categories:

- **a misunderstanding**—a mistake made because he has not understood the information or instruction you gave; for example, the child puts the glue on the top of the cupboard instead of inside —he has confused *on* and *in*;
- **an error in his spoken language**—a mistake in working out the systems that govern the foreign language; for example, the child says *mouses* for the plural of *mouse,* instead of *mice*. These spoken errors are a natural part of the process of learning about a language. They should be welcomed as they show us how the child is getting on and what stage he has gotten to in working out the systems (see page 34);
- **an error in pronunciation**—for example, saying *zee* instead of *the*.

Don't be tempted to say, "You've made a mistake." Deal with mistakes in the same way as you did when you were helping your child with his own language. Repeat what you said again in a soft and kind voice, as if nothing has happened (see page 35).

A misunderstanding

Repeat the instruction: "Look again. You cut here and then you stick it on here." Use more gestures to make understanding easier.

An error in spoken language

Repeat the correct language: "Oh! You ate it." The child will repeat back to you, "Yes, I ate it," having changed the *eated it* to *ate it*. If your child doesn't correct himself, don't be tempted to make some comment. Make sure you do some activity in the next session that uses the same language. If you give him more experience, he will correct himself when he is ready.

An error in pronunciation

Repeat the phrase again: "Yes, it was an elephant." The child will repeat back, correcting *elphant* into *elephant*.

Children learn by working things out by themselves in their own time. So do adults to some degree. Think about changing a flat tire. Not until you've done it once by yourself do you really know how to do it. It may satisfy adults to tell children rules. It makes them feel that they have taught them something. However, progress isn't really made by doing this, as children are not as likely to remember rules if they haven't worked them out for themselves. Once they have worked out the rules, parents can contribute by helping them classify their information into groups or sets.

"What age to begin?"

Where a foreign language is not included in a school curriculum, this has to be a personal decision made by individual families.

In the case of a binational family, each parent might like to use their own language from birth. Many parents feel they cannot manage the other family language in the parentese form. "I can't be warm and soft in English," a Spanish woman said. "No one taught me at school how to do it. I don't know what words to use and I feel Miguel is losing out when I hear his father talking to him so sweetly in English."

In another binational family both parents made a conscious decision to use only one language. When their children were seven and eight, they then decided it was time to start using the second language, but their children objected saying, "What for? We can all speak English." It would have been better to wait for some real purpose before introducing the other language. Fortunately, shortly after this, the Austrian great-aunt wrote saying she was coming to stay for a month. The parents decided to make good use of the visit and started preparing the children. By the time great-aunt arrived, the children were ready to join in games, songs, and simple conversations with her.

The idea "the sooner the better" is not always true. Most young children appear to have no difficulty in absorbing language and imitating pronunciation. From the onset of adolescence, learning language appears to be more difficult. Certainly adolescent feelings and emotions and peer-group opinions make it less easy for them to try out a foreign language. Adolescents seem to be more concerned about making mistakes in front of others than young children.

Ideally, it is better to start well before adolescence so that the child has long enough to establish a good base before he becomes self-conscious. If foreign-language lessons at school begin at ten it may be too late: start something at home before. Ideally, begin when children are less busy at school, for example, in a period when there are no assessments or examinations.

If your child is not very good at using his own language and does not have a good vocabulary, you might be better off to concentrate on sharing reading and developing his own language before you start a foreign language. It is easier for the child if he can read in his own language before he begins reading in a foreign language (see page 122).

If your child is in the middle of learning to read his own language, it might be better to help him regularly with reading before you begin the foreign language at home. If he has already begun a foreign language at school, it's probably better not to spend too much time on the foreign language, but to increase the amount of shared reading time until he can read well.

You may want to start at the age of three or four. This can be fun, but you might find that your child doesn't learn very much in your short shared times, and what he does learn is soon forgotten. If you leave it until your child can read, you'll find that he picks up the same amount in a much shorter time.

Final thoughts

Attitudes and life-long interests are formed before the age of eight or nine. It is important to bear this in mind when you consider helping your child with a foreign language. Through the language your child will find out about a new culture, and if you do it together, he'll reflect your attitudes. You will be his window to a new world.

Time spent in sharing experiences together in preadolescent years is precious and important. Later, in the maturing young adult, you'll see many of these same interests and attitudes reemerge.

CHAPTER FOUR

What do children want to learn in the foreign language?

Children absorb the language of their environment. In learning a foreign language your child will want to talk about the foreign-language environment that you organize for her. If she can't join in simple conversations, she'll find it more difficult to acquire language and progress toward fluency will be slow. You can help her to join in gradually by using parentese language techniques. Don't worry if initially you do most of the talking. It's natural. That's what happened when your baby learned to talk. Your conversations will slowly move toward more equal sharing. Eventually she'll take over running some of the games herself, and you'll be just a player.

Is the language children pick up really useful to them?

Children learn by doing and picking up some of the language that accompanies what they are doing. When activities involve them physically as well as mentally and emotionally, they seem to learn best. Children will pick up whatever foreign language they hear. To begin with, they pick up some single words as well as ready-made or prefabricated phrases. Use phrases to make simple conversations. Children are busy both in school and out, so don't waste their learning time and energy by making them pick up phases that aren't useful to them.

From the child's point of view, why learn, "Les Messieurs font comme ça" (*The gentlemen do like this*) from the famous song "Sur le Pont D'Avignon"? When is a child beginning to learn French going to use such a phrase? Can she transfer it to other situations? It's more worthwhile to teach her a song such as:

Un deux trois, ma boule.
Quatre cinq six qui roule,
Sept huit neuf sur la pelouse,
Dix onze douze, jusqu'à Toulouse.

At least it helps with counting and can be enjoyed by all the family.

The same is true for making her learn adult language such as "I'm very sorry indeed. Please excuse me." Child culture has its own accepted language level—and this isn't it. If a child used it when playing with foreign children, they'd probably make fun of her. This could put her off speaking a foreign language for a long time before her confidence could be rebuilt.

Children expect to speak immediately

Children want to get on quickly and expect instant results. For them that means speaking some foreign language in their first session and being able to show some of it off afterward. In the same way as they learned their own language, reading and writing should come later, once they can speak. Whatever language they pick up, if they're confident and get the chance, they'll not hesitate to use it in an effort to start a conversation.

Japanese primary-school children in Tokyo had picked up This is a pen *from a comic TV Japanese language program. They used it, without knowing its meaning, to initiate conversation with foreigners in the local park. When the foreigners replied, they burst into embarrassed laughter. They couldn't understand a single word of the reply.*

Children find it more difficult to learn words and phrases that are not linked to any activity. Learning a list of vocabulary or individual words for spelling takes a long time, and very soon afterward they've forgotten how to spell most of them. If they're in context they're much more likely to remember them.

Help from a "friend"

It doesn't occur to many adults that some children can't visualize a conversation in a foreign language. They can't imagine how the foreign language goes back and forth from one person to another. Before they've the confidence to try themselves, they need to see and hear a conversation. You may be able to show your child examples of foreign-language speakers talking on video, but if this uses complicated language, it's better to try another method. You don't want to discourage her.

One way of helping your child over this difficulty is to introduce a new and special character who speaks only the foreign language—a French or Italian doll, a Spanish puppet, or German toy dog. Through your "friend" you can target exactly the language you need. You can have fun, too. Use a different tone of voice for your new friend, invent stories about him, and even make him do amusing as well as naughty things. Conversations between you and your friend can develop into conversations between him and your child and eventually into three-way discussions. Let your friend join in games, too. A third player can make a game more exciting: two is slightly limiting.

"It's your turn, Hans," Mother says to the German toy dog.
"Woof, woof. My turn. Woof. Have you got a six, James? Yes or no?"

the German dog, Hans, asks.
James replies, "Yes, Hans. I have. Here it is," giving the card to
Hans.
"Thanks," says Hans. "I've got a pair. Look, two sixes. My turn
again. Woof, woof. Who shall I ask this time? James or Mom? Woof,
woof, woof." (followed by a pause to add suspense) "James. Have
you got a ten?"
"No, I haven't, Hans. Now it's my turn."

In some families the relationship with the friend develops so well that he becomes an adopted member of the family. He's even given his own clothes, hair brush, bed, and food, and all the family know his likes and dislikes. Step by step a whole foreign-language world has been built around him. Packing his bag for him to go away for the weekend with the family involves using a lot of foreign language, especially if you're not going to forget something!

What do children want to talk about in a foreign language?

Children need language to talk about:
- themselves;
- their families;
- their interests;
- their daily needs;
- their life—what they did and are going to do;
- their surroundings;
- their feelings;
- their likes and dislikes;
- their thoughts and opinions;
- their troubles.

Children also want language to be able to:

- understand what others say about these topics;
- ask questions about these topics and understand the answers.

Without this language they find it difficult to start off conversations and keep them going.

- Children need specific foreign language for coping with everyday life.

If you want your child to get used to speaking the foreign language only when you're doing things together, you have to help her build up her own bank of useful prefabricated phrases. From understanding and using simple phrases, she'll progress to creating partially prefabricated phrases. Very much later, after she has had plenty of experience, she'll begin to create her own speech (see page 44). Initially it will be you who uses the prefabricated phrases.

Specific language (useful prefabricated phrases)

Survival language	I don't understand. Say it again. How do I do it?
Transactional language	Please give me the scissors. Pass the glue.
Socializing language	Can I play? You can share with me.
Management language	For organizing: • Foreign Language Time (see page 71); • self-study, including reading and writing; • projects and activities; • drawing and crafts; • games.

The value of checklists

These checklists (pages 64 to 67) may look daunting, but they're only a guide to help you check that as your child progresses, you are exposing her to all the types of language she needs. Your child needs a complete menu of language if she is going to carry on normally and express herself. If she can't talk about something that is important to her when everyone around her speaks only the foreign language, she could be embarrassed and frustrated, too.

> *Invited to an American home for a birthday party, a little Japanese boy, who had arrived three weeks previously, didn't know the language to ask to go to the toilet. He knew that if he said **Please**, people at school tried to figure out what he wanted. The parents, however, thought he was being very polite and that was all. The situation was saved when, eventually, they all went out to play and without saying anything, he conveniently ran behind a bush.*

In fact, if you look at the lists carefully, you'll see that they include many of the things any child of four or five uses or understands, but at a simple level. Don't try to use complicated language forms when your child is just beginning. Think back to when she started to speak. She used very simple language at first.

To introduce language for feelings, you can begin with "I'm hot" and "I'm cold." When your child understands these phrases, introduce "I'm tired," "I'm sleepy."

Then play a simple game. The first player mimes something, and the second player asks "What's the matter?" and then guesses, saying "Are you sleepy?" "No," replies the first player and repeats the mime. "Oh, you're hot," the second player says. "Yes, that's right. I'm hot," the second player says. The players then change roles. For children who might find this difficult, Mom and the "friend" can play the game first to show how to play and what language to use (see page 58).

What language does the parent need?

(See the Appendix on page 194 for foreign language phrases.) Language is needed for:

- **Questions**—Closed questions that give yes or no replies: "Is it red?" Open questions: "How did you do it?" "What did you do next?" "And then?"
- **Suggestions**—"Do you want . . . ?"
- **Discussions and negotiations**—"Why do you think . . . ?" "Have you got an idea?"
- **Explanations and justifications**—"This is red." "The line's here, so cut here."
- **Discipline and instructions**—"Don't do that now." "Tidy up."
- **Encouragement and praise**—"That's nearly right, try again." "Well done."

Parentese techniques can be operated within these types of language.

Select language to fit situations

Random choice of language to fit activities may result in children not having all the language forms they need. For this reason it is a good idea for the adult to refer to a hidden syllabus. This syllabus provides:

- a check on what language has been used;

- an aid to planning what needs to be introduced.

It appears that all children go through the same sequence in language learning even if their cultural background and the language they hear around them is different. Children acquire grammatical structures in a relatively predictable order. It used to be thought that the past tense should be left until the child had studied a foreign language for about two years. In fact, many foreign-language textbooks didn't introduce the past tense until the third level, although children had been using the past tense from a very early age in their own language.

Children like and need to talk about what they did and what happened in their life. It is important to them, and it is something they do well in their own language.

A girl aged 11 returning from an exchange with a French family was asked by her eager parents, "Did you speak a lot of French?" "How could I," the girl replied. "I could only talk about things happening here and now like 'I'm eating bread and drinking milk,' and that was obvious. They could see what I was doing. I wanted to tell them about places I'd visited and what I'd done, but I couldn't. I didn't know how. My teacher hadn't taught me. So I didn't say anything."

A suggested hidden syllabus

This checklist:

- is a guide for use in recording and planning;
- outlines the basic categories needed by young children;
- is compiled using English and needs to be adapted to match foreign languages;
- is not listed in any specific order.

Item	Examples	Accompanying question
Numbers		*How many? How much?*
Alphabet		
Colors	*brown, blue, green, orange, etc.*	*What color is this/that?*
Nouns	• classification (some things are uncountable like water)	*What's this?*
	• with indefinite article *(the)*	*Where's the . . . ?*
	• plural forms	*How many are there?*
Conjunctions	*and, or*	*Is this a . . . or a . . . ?*
Verbs	to be *(I am . . .),* to have got *(I've got . .)* simple present	affirmative and negative question forms (Are you? Aren't you?)
Prepositions of place	*in, on, under, near*	*Where is it? Where are they?*

Imperatives for instructions	*Stop, Go up, Turn right/left* (affirmative)	
	Don't stop, Don't turn right (negative)	
Adjectives	*big, little, sad, happy,* etc.	
Pronouns		
Subject pronouns	*I, you, he, she, we, you, they*	*Who*
Possessive pronouns	*my, yours, his, hers, its, ours, theirs*	*Whose?*
Verbs	want + noun *want an apple, don't want an apple*	
	want + infinitive *want to go, don't want to go*	*Are we going?*
Verbs	can + infinitive *can run, can jump, can't run*	*Is he running?*
Verbs	like + noun *like bananas, like ice cream, don't like bananas*	*Do you like bananas?*
	like + verb *like playing the piano, don't like playing the piano*	*Does she like playing the piano?*

Item	Examples	Accompanying question
Time	days of the week parts of the day (*morning, afternoon, evening, night*) meal times hours and minutes seasons	*When?* *What time is it?*
Nouns for the family	*mother, father, sister, brother,* etc.	*Who is . . . ?*
Nouns for parts of the body	*leg, arm, head,* etc.	
Nouns for clothes	*T-shirt, dress*	*Whose is . . . ?*
Nouns for home	rooms (*kitchen*, etc.), furniture (*sofa, bed,* etc.)	
Prepositions for transport	*by bus, on foot*	*How did you go?*

Classifiers	*a piece of, a bottle of, a glass of,*		
	a box of, etc.		
Verb forms	**affirmative**	**negative**	**question form**
Present continuous	*I am eating*	*I am not going*	*Are you listening?*
Simple past	*I went*	*He didn't come*	*Did you win?*
Future	*He will buy*	*I won't go*	*Will you ask?*
Professions	*a doctor*		*What is he/she?*
			What are they?
Places	*station, supermarket, hospital*		*Where is . . .?*
			Where does he work?
Adverbs	*slowly, quickly*		*How?*
	now, soon, sometimes		*When?*
	here, there		*Where?*
Adjectives			
Comparative	*smaller*		*Which is smaller?*
Superlative	*smallest*		*Which is the smallest?*
Irregular adjectives	*good, better, best*		*Which is the smallest?*

Introduction of items

Items should be introduced slowly, step by step.

Play the card game "What color is it?" (see page 92). Two colors are introduced to begin with, and later a third is added. The second time the game is played, the same three colors are used again, and then a further two colors are introduced, making five colors in all.

The next time the game is played, if the child knows all five colors, one or two more new colors are introduced.

Every time the game is played, the same game language is used for organizing the game. Initially this game is played with colored cards.

At a later stage, colors are replaced by words for colors.

Questions parents ask

"What do I do if I find on checking the hidden syllabus that I've missed an item?"

Build an activity or a game around the item and introduce it that way. The same game can often be adapted for using different language items. If your child already knows how to play the game, she can concentrate on the new language.

"How can I get more information on hidden syllabus items in the foreign language?"

Buy a textbook for beginners. If it's an adult textbook, remember that some of the colloquial language may not be children's language. Check the list in the appendix for basic foreign-language items.

69

WHAT DO CHIDREN WANT TO LEARN IN THE FOREIGN LANGUAGE?

Final thoughts

Planning what foreign language to use is as important as planning how and when to use it. If you learned a foreign language at school, even for a short time, you'll already be familiar with a lot of the hidden syllabus your child will need.

Thinking carefully about what foreign language to use, and talking about it with your child when an opportunity arises, is not a waste of time for either of you. Getting to know how another language works helps you to know more about your own and ultimately to use it better.

> *"He who knows no foreign language does not truly know his own."*
> *(Goethe, 1749–1832)*

Planning—Types of help

How can I help?

You are the key to your child's success. You can make learning happen. However small your contribution, as long as it is fun for both of you, you'll make a significant impact on your child. Even if you don't feel confident about your ability in the foreign language, your help and support will give him the confidence to start and then go further and find out more for himself.

Your child will be motivated by your:

- interest;
- patient guidance;
- encouragement and praise.

Your child will learn easily and quickly if you plan and select carefully so that his learning time isn't misused or wasted. This means planning both:

- the activities;
- the language used in them.

What type of help should I give?

Ideally, a weekly commitment would include one or more of the following during the school year. Don't try to continue the same pattern during the school holidays. A different and more relaxed atmosphere prevails in the home then, and it's pointless to fight against it.

Language Time

For example, "Spanish Time" or "German Time":

- duration about ten minutes each time
- once, twice, or three times a week or to fit in with school homework nights
- time and place—the same each day and known in advance by the child

Language Time should be planned by you to slot different activities into the routine framework (see page 77). Homework can be one of these activities.

Informal Shorties

- informal learning times
- duration from few minutes up to ten minutes
- spontaneous—at no fixed time

This is a spontaneous switch into the foreign language, initiated by you to catch a mood or follow up an interest shown by your child or the family.

Your child begins to hum a foreign-language song. You join in singing the words. You continue with other songs, rhymes, and chants to make a sing-along lasting about four or five minutes. Possibly, you take turns choosing the next song or songs. You stop before the excitement fades.

Planned Shorties

- regular planned short learning times
- duration from five to ten minutes

A Planned Shortie is planned by you to consolidate something you've done in Language Time or to share a book, song, or rhyme.

When your child is in bed, you put on a cassette of a story in the foreign language and let him fall asleep listening to the cassette.

Introduce the family's "foreign friend" for a quick conversation with some other member of the family.

Projects

- at no fixed time
- sessions lasting from ten to thirty minutes over several days or weeks, depending on the project

Projects are planned by you with some special aim:
—A meal in a Thai restaurant. Prepare beforehand and follow up afterwards.
—A visit to a supermarket to collect as many French words as possible.

Child Times

- lasting from five to fifteen minutes
- initiated by your child asking you to do something with him

Requests like this may throw off your plans. However, it's important to respond positively and give him your undivided attention. His request shows that he's ready to learn. At times like this he'll absorb language easily and fast. Don't miss this sort of opportunity and remember—he'll note your reaction.

"Can you play snap with me? I've put the cards out," Tina, aged 9, asked her mother. Her mother switched off the cooking and settled down with her. The phone rang but she didn't answer it. They just got on with the game until it was finished. It took about five minutes.

Language Corner (German Corner, Chinese Corner, French Corner, etc.)

- continuous
- a family enterprise

The German Corner wasn't in fact a corner. It was a small table and bookcase in the hall accessible to all the family. Everything on the table and pinned to the bulletin board above the table was about German language and culture. Books including dictionaries, games, audiocassettes, videos, and other reference material were kept in the bookcase. It was a mini-resource center. Dan's German writing and games he'd made were regularly displayed there, too. In this way all the family could see what he and Mom had been doing together.

Making a mini-resource center focusing on the language not only helps to keep interest alive, it also saves time spent in looking for things. If a child can't find something right away, he loses interest. By the time he's found it, he's probably already thinking about something else, and a learning opportunity has been lost.

Some exhibits need to be changed each week if interest is to be continually restimulated for everyone. Some things in the Language Corner can also interest visitors. If this happens, don't be tempted to make the explanation yourself: leave it to your child. To have to explain something is a good way of finding out what you really know. Don't be surprised if in the middle of the explanation you get asked, "What's this again, Dad?" Take it as a chance to retell him. Don't be tempted to make any remark, even a joke, about the fact that he's forgotten. A remark like that wouldn't contribute anything and might inhibit him from explaining something the next time an occasion arises.

A bi-national American Korean boy at College explained that until he was seven he only spoke English at home with his American mother and Korean father. Once he went to school, he began to pick up some Korean from other kids in his class. When he spoke Korean with his father, his father criticized his pronunciation and mistakes in grammar. After a while, he gave up speaking Korean at home and only spoke it when he went to his Korean grandparents, as they encouraged him.

Extending learning into the family

Children like to feel secure and know what is expected of them. The regular program of Language Times when your child has your attention to himself provides him with an ideal learning environment. If he knows that what you do together in Language Times can be shared in fun ways at other times with the rest of the family, he'll feel proud and more confident about what he is doing.

Keeping the interest going

Once you have started to help with a foreign language, you may find that for some valid reason you can't continue regular Language Times. Since your family has gotten into the habit of using a little foreign language, don't let it drop. Give your child some valid reason for abandoning Language Times but keep some Shorties. Keep the Language Corner as well. Pick up new pictures from magazines or buy a box of something to eat from Spain or Germany. It is so important to keep the little language you can all use alive. Beginning a second time is not the same. Something of the initial spark is no longer there, and learning may be more of a task.

There may be times when you or your child seem to be losing enthusiasm. It's quite natural. We all have ups and downs. It's essential to get out of the down before it does too much damage.

Think of something special to do such as celebrating a festival, an outing on which you invite one of his friends, or a new book or a video. They'll help change the atmosphere, especially if you inject some excitement through your use of language (see page 26). It's a good idea to keep one or two things in reserve, ready for the rainy day when he might need that extra boost (see page 59).

When either of you are feeling down, it's a good time to show him some of the work you did a month or two before. Both of you will be pleased to see how much progress he's made. It's good to do a little self-evaluation. Success stimulates. It's also good to know that you might be able to do a little better. Don't be tempted to tell him. He'll know himself, and probably you'll find he'll soon improve.

How do I plan?

You are the manager and facilitator of all learning, even if it is in reaction to your child's request (see page 72). It is up to you to select the activities you do and guide the language you use in them. You in fact guide total immersion for your child (see page 51).

If you plan carefully, and also give time and thought as to how best to follow up, things will run more smoothly. You'll also feel much more confident. Being sure of what you intend to do enables you to be more flexible and make use of opportunities to be more creative should they arise.

Random decisions about what you are going to do in Language Time just a few minutes before you begin may not always turn out to be as effective as you had hoped. This doesn't mean that you shouldn't feel free to alter your plans if your child has a really good idea or you or he happen to feel lackluster. It is important to be flexible and react to situations. What you've planned won't be wasted. You can always use it on another day.

Once you get into the rhythm of regularly helping your child, you'll find that you'll be planning and collecting things as you go about your daily life (see page 158). You may find that you collect so much that you have to select what you introduce and when. Don't fall into the trap of presenting too many materials and not enough language to go with them. If the accompanying language isn't presented and practiced effectively, which takes time, a potential language-learning opportunity will be missed, although other things may have been learned and you'll have had fun.

Overall plan

Be clear as to:

- **your long-term targets in language and also culture.** Ask yourself "What for?" "By when?"
- **the length of time to be spent in Language Times.** Ask yourself, "When and how long each week?" "For what length of time—a semester or the winter?"
- **what materials to use?** Ask yourself, "Where shall I obtain materials?" "Where should I put a Language Corner?"

Monthly or two-weekly plan

It is much easier to plan if you break learning targets into small and more manageable blocks.

These may include:

- types of activities (see chapters 6 and 8);
- language content for you as manager and facilitator of activities;
- language content for your child:
  —listening and understanding (see chapter 4);
  —speaking;
  —reading and writing (see chapter 7);
- cultural information (see chapter 11);
- materials such as videos, cassettes, props, realia, and visuals (see chapter 9).

Weekly plan

- Plan and estimate the time and place of Language Times.
- Map out rough plans for Language Times. These will need to be adapted after each Language Time. Prepare more material than you may actually use. You never know beforehand how long a game may take or whether an idea will work. For this reason it's advisable to have a reserve just in case you need to change your plan.
- Once you have planned Language Time for a week, work out when to fit in Planned Shorties.
- During the holidays, it's important to continue, but, instead of Language Time, increase the number of Planned Shorties and introduce a big project or several shorter projects.

Language Time program

The framework of the program stays the same. Activities are slotted into each section.

Suggested program:
- Warm-up;
- New language presentation;
- Reading and writing activity or homework (if appropriate);
- Game or crafts for language practice;
- Ending.

The time spent on each section is flexible. Be prepared to shorten or lengthen them to fit your overall program or a special occasion. Adjust them on the spot to match the mood of your child and his ability to concentrate on that day. Excitement at school, a slight cold, or even a change in the weather can alter your child's ability to concentrate. To push him beyond what he can take can be counterproductive. If you make adjustments without changing the framework, your child will get to know the routine. He'll even predict what's next. Some children know the routine so well that they're to be found making preparations for the next step before it's been suggested.

Each Language Time should include:

- presentation of new language;
- practice of familiar language.

Without opportunities to practice the language that you've already presented and he's understood, your child can't absorb it. If he doesn't get sufficient opportunities to consolidate through practice, he won't reach the stage when he can use the language himself. When he was learning his own language, you presented new language to him and made sure he understood it. Then you gave him opportunities to use the same language again and again in natural ways within the different activities you arranged for him. You can help him again if you use some of these same parentese techniques in well-selected activities (see page 24).

Opportunities to practice language using parentese techniques occur in:

- getting ready to begin, tidying up, etc.;
- organizing games, handwork, activities, projects;
- social situations;
- organizing sing-along rhymes, songs, chants, etc.

Warm-up

The transition to using a foreign language is difficult for some children, especially as it happens at home where there is no obvious communicative reason or change in circumstances to make it necessary. Although you may think that your child takes it in his stride, it's still a good idea to help make the transition, as this should speed up actual learning.

Before you sit down together to start Language Time, put on a cassette of foreign-language songs or music associated with the country. It helps to set the scene and create an atmosphere. Then warm up with a sing-along that includes rhymes and chants as well as songs, some with physical actions, that you both know. This will help to tune both of you in to listening to the foreign language and get you in the mood for talking.

Slot part of a verse of a new song or rhyme into the sing-along each Language Time so that you continually increase your repertoire (see page 120).

Presentation of new language

Informal presentation

When your child was learning his own language, you presented new language in a natural way while he was involved in doing something. You had no conscious plan. You can continue to do this with a foreign language as long as you don't present too much at any one time and make sure that it is linked to an activity.

Formal presentation

However, as your child is now older, time is limited, and he expects immediate results. You'll find it more effective to plan a regular presentation of new language in Language Time.

It is easier to help your child now than when he was learning his own language. If you select activities that he already knows and understands, you have only to help him with one thing—a new language (see page 44).

Wherever possible, begin by going over familiar language and build the new language on to this. You may like to use your "friend" to help. As when your child was in the early stages of learning his own language, make sure that you repeat the new language several times without rewording it or expanding it. Place yourself in a position where your child can see your mouth movements, as he is used to using them as clues to learning language (see page 26).

An example of a formal presentation

Step 1: Present new language

Add the new language on to some language your child already knows.

> **Familiar language:** This is a bus and this is a car.
> **New language:** and this is a bicycle . . . a bicycle . . . a bicycle
> and this is a van . . . a van . . . a van

Accompany this by realia (a toy car), pictures, and body language.

By building on to familiar language, you get an opportunity to revise it, which helps learning.

At this stage, don't ask your child to say anything. The new language is backed by concrete examples or pictures. At this stage there is no written text and so no reading in the foreign language (see chapter 7).

Step 2: Check to ensure that understanding has taken place

Say, "Point to a van" or "Show me a van." Wait to see if your child does it correctly. If he does, praise him. If he makes a mistake, re-present the new language again as in step 1. Continue saying, "Point to a bicycle" or "Show me a bicycle." At the end of the session, again ask your child any things you had to re-present.

When you play this again at a later stage, vary the language and say, "Which is the bicycle?"

If you feel that your child can take on more new language, go back to step 1 and introduce two more items. But don't be over-ambitious and push too far. As he gets more used to the foreign language he will be able to absorb new language more quickly.

Steps 1 and 2 take place in the same Language Time.

Step 3: Practice language

When you have built up the number of items over several Language Times and have accumulated enough, play Lotto (see page 107) using them.

> Parent: *a bicycle* *Have you got it?*
> Child: *a bicycle* *Yes. Me.* *No*

Playing Lotto lasts over several Language Times. Build in new items once you have presented them.

Step 4: The child uses the language himself

Spread all the cards picture upward on a surface. Point to an item and ask, "What's this?" pointing to a bicycle. Your child replies, "It's a bicycle." Continue asking every item in turn. If he gets a card right, he can pick it up.

To show your child what language to use, run the dialogue through with the "friend," before you ask him. If your child can't give you an answer, repeat it for him using a soft whisper slowly (parentese techniques). Later, let him try again. Children like to have a second chance. If he still can't manage it, repeat it again and encourage him. He obviously needs more practice.

After you have checked that he can use the language, play other games to give him additional practice (see page 105).

Reading and writing

This should be optional and depends on your child's:

- level in his own language;
- ability to speak in the foreign language.

As in learning his own language, reading and writing should come once he can speak.

If he has foreign-language homework, slot it into Language Time at this point. Your child will be better prepared for doing his school or club homework if he has had an oral warm-up and you have been able to re-present some of the language involved orally before he reads and writes it.

Games and crafts

The selection of these is closely linked to the new language, as the aim is to provide opportunities to practice it. Language used in these activities should already be familiar. New language that has just been presented shouldn't be practiced in the same Language Time. It seems that for learning to take place there should be a time lag between the introduction of new language and practicing it.

> *Having introduced things seen in the street (shops, people, cars, etc.) and played Lotto (see page 107) using them, one parent made an outline drawing of a street and asked her child to stick or draw the same things on it. She also asked her to add traffic lights and a crossing. Making this picture spread over four Language Times. As the picture developed, her child suggested additional things and even put the national flag fluttering over the railway station. This picture was then displayed in the Language Corner, and after several family discussions, she added some more items.*

Ending

Tidying up is often done quickly and with little language. In actual fact, tidying can provide an ideal opportunity to reintroduce or check new language. To begin with, you will have to do all the talking.

> Parent: *"Give me the red crayon. Now give me the green crayon. Thank you. Now the orange one. How many have I got? Let's count them."*
>
> Together: *"One, two, three."*

It is good to sum up what you have done in a Language Time. For example, look at the picture, admire it and discuss what could be added next time.

Finally, before you stop, repeat the new rhyme, chant, or song and then say *goodbye* to the "friend," if you have one, and return him to his home.

Concentration

It is important that one activity in Language Time flows into another. If you keep up the momentum and fun, your child will be involved and concentrating on what he's doing. If you have gaps when you are looking for something you need, you'll lose his interest, and concentration will go. It may be difficult to get it back.

As your child is working in a foreign language, his concentration span is likely to be shorter than when he's doing the same sort of thing using his own language. Although you want to encourage him to stick at something and persevere, it's pointless to push an activity once interest has been lost. For this reason it's important to prepare more activities than you would for a similar length of time when your child is using his own language.

Planning language

Since the aim of any activity is to practice language at the same time as doing something purposeful, it is important to plan what language you want to use. In doing the activity, your child will be totally immersed in the foreign language. Learning it will be made easier because you have planned it—you've provided him with guided total immersion activities (see page 51). Without planning the use of language, progression is slower.

Without a plan it is more difficult:

- to build on familiar language;
- to introduce effective practice;
- to limit your own language to what the child needs.

Where language content has not been planned, your child may

find himself confused by language that is too complicated for his stage of learning. It's very easy for adults to use too much and too difficult language. If language, foreign or his own, is way beyond a child's understanding, he switches off. To plan well, you may find it helpful to think back to how you used parentese techniques.

> *An American boy aged eight attending a Spanish class after school boasted to his mother that he and his friends had a great time. Señora spoke English in such a funny way, they couldn't understand what she said, so they did what they wanted. Obviously, the boys had given up listening. When the mother checked how much Spanish they actually had picked up, she was very disappointed.*

Assessment and follow-up

After Language Time, assess what you have achieved and make notes on what needs doing again or can be shared with the family. These few quick notes help in planning the next Language Time and targeting consolidation. If possible, make these notes as soon as you've finished. If you leave it until later, you'll find that some things have already slipped your memory.

Questions parents ask

"My child doesn't know much about foreign languages. What should I do before I begin?"

Make sure your child knows and understands:

Why he is going to learn a foreign language.

When—explain about Language Times and make a Language Corner together. Introduce him to some things linked to the foreign language. As you do this, explain where the language is spoken and by whom. Tell him who in your family or friends can also speak it.

How—explain that learning will include fun activities and projects for him and the family. Explain that you will be talking to him in the foreign language and he should try and say some things in the foreign language, too.

"How much of his own language should I use? When should I translate?"

As soon as possible you should provide guided total-immersion experiences for your child. This means using only the foreign language and helping your child to get used to understanding by gist. He knows how to do this. He does it in his own language (see page 31).

In the first Language Time, you may have to translate most things. But don't let this become a habit, as he'll learn to wait for your translation and not make any effort to understand or even listen properly to the foreign language. When you find you have to translate something, do it in a stage whisper so that he realizes it is something special and not a regular thing. Don't translate word for word either, as he'll get used to wanting to know what every single word means, and this is something you're trying to discourage. Until he gets used to understanding by gist, he can't make progress.

When you introduce something new, use some realia or a picture accompanied by parentese techniques to help him understand—just as you did when he was learning to speak (see page 23). If you think it is really necessary, tell him once in both languages, but after that only use the foreign language.

Discussions about culture need a lot of language and involve new concepts, so initially they have to take place in your own language. Since you are working toward using only the foreign language during Language Times and Planned Shorties it is better to arrange for this sort of discussion to take place at other times. Start them off when both of you are looking at a new picture or exhibit in the Language Corner. If there are any words you want him to know in the foreign language, you can introduce them into your conversation; for example, "This is called *ein . . .* in German."

"How do I help him to make progress?"

Virtually all children make some degree of progress. Since learning is a continuous process, it is difficult to assess progress accurately; some language learned might not be used until a much later stage.

Your child will progress if he's having fun and you:

- plan what language to introduce (see page 62);
- present and practice language using parentese techniques in selected purposeful activities;
- show enthusiasm, have fun, and are positive about what you and he are doing.

"What do I do if he isn't interested?"

Assess what you are doing. Are you getting it right?

- Is it fun?
- Are you using language he can use?
- Is it purposeful?
- Can he and others see his progress? Are you providing him with opportunities to show off his attainments?

Remotivate him by some exciting new project.

"What language do I need for organizing Language Time?"

Use the same language each time and gradually build on it as you did when your child was learning to speak. Check the language for organizing activities and games (see page 103). You will notice that much of it recurs, especially in games.

Progression of language

Put it there. → Put it there on the chair. → Put it on the chair
by the window.

Get a red one. → Get a red one and a
green one, too.

"How do I start off with a seven-year-old?"

Begin with something you feel confident about and something easy that you know your child can use and will have fun using.

The first Language Time might consist of learning numbers. Your child may already know some numbers in the foreign language; if this is the case, re-present them and then build new numbers onto the familiar numbers. Whether you are starting from nothing or building onto familiar language, don't do more than he can manage successfully.

During the first few Language Times, you'll have very little foreign language you can use and that he understands. Transfer these words and phrases to different situations, just in the same way as your child did when he was learning to talk (see page 23). Hearing them over and over again helps learning.

First impressions are important and lasting. They influence attitudes, so it is vital that your child ends the first Language Time:

- feeling positive about learning a foreign language;
- being capable of showing off some foreign-language words;
- wanting to learn more;
- looking forward to the next Language Time.

The praise and admiration he gets from others—adults and other children—for his new language skills are crucial for self-motivation.

PART 2

Planning—Starting off a program

Ideas for a first Language Time

Warm-up

- Play a cassette of children singing in the foreign language.

New language presentation

- Start with the numbers 1, 2, 3. First find out if your child knows any numbers in the new language. Then present or build onto these numbers using numbers cards.

Step 1

Showing the card ⓵, say in the foreign language "one" and repeat "one." Make sure that he can see your face clearly so that he can watch as well as hear the word. At this stage, do not ask your child to say the word, though you may find that he begins to mouth the word without actually saying it. Repeat step 1, introducing "two" 2 and "three." 3

Step 2

Put the cards number upwards on a flat surface and say, "Show me *one*" and then "Show me *two*" and "Show me *three*." Praise him if he gets them right. Re-present them if he makes a mistake.

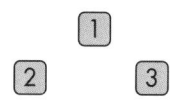

Games

- *Stand-on game*

  Place large number cards on the floor. Say "three" and show your child that you want him to stand on that number. Play a game with the other numbers in the same way saying, "Stand on (pause to add suspense) . . . *three*." Repeat using all the numbers. Continue as long as it is fun.

- *How many?*

  Ask your child to hold up the correct number of fingers. Say, "Show me *three*." If he holds up three fingers, say "Yes, *three*. Good." Or, if not, "No, look," and show him three fingers while saying "three."

Crafts

Number cards

- Make two sets of number cards together. Color the numbers red or blue.
- Present new language (*some paper, scissors*) and two colored pens (*red* and *blue*) and use phrases such as "Give me the scissors" and "Copy this." Collect the cards together

in packs and say, "Give me one." "Give me two." "Give me three."

Chant

- Make up a chant using the numbers you have introduced. Clap or stamp your feet to the rhythm.

One, two, three,
Three, three, three.

Extension into the family

- Do the chant together.
- Play the number game with fingers together.

Ideas for the second Language Time

Warm-up

- Use the cassette as in the first Language Time.
- Say the number chant.

New language presentation

Re-present the numbers used last time and present the new numbers, *four* and *five*.

Crafts

Make new cards for *four* and *five* [4] [5] and make two boards for Lotto. Use number symbols to begin with, and when your child is ready to start reading, gradually swap the symbol for the number word . [4] [four]

Re-present *scissors*, etc., and add two new colors: *green* and *yellow*.

Game

- *Lotto*

  Introduce the following new language:

  Parent: *"Five."* (*holding up the card*) *"Have you got five? Five."*

  Child: *"Five. Yes. Me." or "No."*

  Parent: *"Five. Yes. Me. I've got it." or "Five. No."*

- *Quick game—Guess the number*

  Hide a number card ⬚3⬚ behind your back and say, "How many?" and let your child guess. If he can't say the number, he can show you the corresponding card. After a pause to add suspense, show the card and repeat "How many?" If he can't manage, help him by mouthing the reply. If he's right he keeps the card. If he makes a mistake, you keep the card and use it again toward the end of the game. Repeat using all the numbers. Count his cards together at the end of the game.

Ending

- Chant "One, two, three" and add on "four" and "five."

Extension into the family

- Chant, count together, and play Lotto.

The third Language Time

Warm-up

- Play the sing-along program.
- Practice the number chant.
- Count numbers together.

New language presentation

- Re-present the numbers *one* to *five* and present the new numbers *six*, *seven*, and *eight* as before.

Crafts

- *Color cards*
  Make some color cards—two cards for each color (red, green, yellow, and blue). Re-present the colors. Introduce "Draw around this (a circle)" and "Color this red," and re-use previous phrases.

Game

- *Memory game*
  Color cards are placed color downward. The first player points to a card and says, "What's this?" He picks it up and says the color, for example, "red." He then points to another card and says, "What's this?" He picks it up and says the color. If the two colors are the same, he keeps the cards. If they are different, he replaces the cards. The next player does exactly the same and the game continues until all the cards have been picked up. To begin with, your child may not be able to say, "What's this?" so say it together. When all the cards have been picked up, count your cards aloud. The winner has the most cards.

- *Quick game*
  Play the stand-on game with the number cards *one* to *five*.

Ending

- Make your own color chant.

  Red, blue, yellow, green.
  Red, blue, yellow, green.

- Count together up to eight and repeat.

Extension into the family

Chant together and play the memory game.

The fourth Language Time

Warm-up

- Play the sing-along program.
- Practice the number chant.
- Practice the color chant.
- Count together to eight.

New language presentation

- Add the new numbers *nine* and *ten*.
- Introduce three pictures of animals.
- Introduce new language: "Look. This is an elephant."
  Repeat *an elephant*. Mime an elephant. "And this is a cat.
  And this is a dog."
     Then ask, "Show me the dog," etc., and mime each ani-
  mal or make each animal's noise in the foreign language.
  (Animal noises generally differ from language to language.)

Crafts

- Make new number cards *six* to *ten,* and two new boards for
  Lotto.

Game

- Play Lotto with numbers *one* to *ten.*

- *Quick game*
  Place the color cards on the floor and play the stand-on game, standing on a color.

  "Stand on . . . red." "Stand on . . . blue."

End

- Mime the animals and say, "This is an elephant," etc.
- Practice the color chant.
- Count to ten together.

Extension into the family

- Count to ten and play Lotto.

The fifth Language Time (revision)

This is compiled from what you have done so far. This gives your child time for extra practice and a feeling that he already knows a lot.

After you have sung or chanted something together, let him repeat part of it by himself, finish off a line of a rhyme, or count in turns, you saying, "one," he "two," and you "three." You may have to help him the first few times by whispering what you want him to say.

The sixth to ninth Language Times

Plan

- Present three more animals. Practice the memory game with animals.

- Present the colors orange and brown.

- Practice them in the memory game and the stand-on game.

- Present nouns of things around you, such as *a chair* and *a table* in preparation for playing a Hide and Seek game. You will need to introduce the language "What's this? It's a . . ."

- Present *on* and *under*. Practice them in a simple game. Using a toy teddy bear, say "Put Teddy on the chair" and extend this to the table, floor, etc. "Yes. Teddy's on the chair." Use gesture to help understanding. If your child makes a mistake, repeat "on the chair" while pointing.

- Develop this into a Hide and Seek game. Hide Teddy yourself so that you can match Teddy's position with the language you are practicing. New language will include "Shut your eyes. Count to ten. Open your eyes. Where's Teddy? Find Teddy." When Teddy is found, repeat, "Look, Teddy's under the table." If appropriate, add on "Hi, Teddy. How are you?"

- Transfer this language to other situations: "Where's . . . ? Look on the chair. Under the book."

The tenth Language Time

Revision.

The eleventh to fourteenth Language Times

Plan

- Present three new animals. Practice them in the memory game.
- Present the names of the parts of the face.
- Practice them in the game Simon Says (see page 106).
- For crafts, make a puppet (its face only).

- Present the new numbers 20, 30, 40, 50, 60, 70, 80, 90, and 100.
- Practice them in the Stand-on game.

The fifteenth Language Time

Revision.

The sixteenth to nineteenth Language Times

Plan

- Present the plurals of animals (*cat/cats*, etc.).
- Practice the memory game with this extended language. Add "two elephants," as the player puts two cards together.

- Present *in* and *by*.
- Practice them in the Hide and Seek game.

- Present *arms*, *legs*, *hands*, *feet*, and *body*.
- Practice them in the Funny Clowns game (see page 108).

The twentieth Language Time

Revision.

Final thoughts

It's you who can make learning a foreign language and finding out about a foreign culture happen. You can open up a new world for your child. If he's already begun, you can make sure it's going to be a success and take him even further. You may not realize it, but you can help your child do something he didn't know he had it in him to do. With your help he will find out that he can use a foreign language to say some of the same things he can say in his own.

Through sharing activities with him and showing him how to do things, he's learning how to do things himself and to check what he's doing. At the same time he's learning how to concentrate and persevere. In fact, he's learning how to learn at the same time as he's learning a foreign language and about a foreign culture.

CHAPTER SIX

Building up spoken fluency —activities, games, songs, rhymes, and chants

What is a game?

In the child's mind there is little difference between a game and an activity to which you have added elements of fun, suspense, and maybe even competition. To the child both are play. A game is play that has been formally structured and institutionalized. The rules are known. Lotto is a game, but what is the difference between Lotto and a board game you and your child make up as an activity?

Games and gamelike activities play an important role in helping your child to learn a foreign language, providing they include sufficient language of the right kind. You should use language in the same ways as you used it when she was learning to speak, but of course adapted, as she's older now.

Although you use language for communicating information, the balance between it and the activity has to be right. Neither should dominate. Activities should not take too much of the limited time. It may be better to do some of the time-consuming cutting beforehand so that you can get on with the part that involves useful language.

A girl who was seven years old and was learning English spent ten minutes of English Time coloring a full-page drawing using no English at all. When it was finished, the parent said "Good. That's nice."

A boy, aged eight, was cutting pictures of cars from a magazine and was bombarded by the parent's untargeted complex language all the time he was cutting and sticking. There was no silence for reflection nor opportunity for him to join in or begin a conversation. He actually seemed to stop listening and let the activity take over.

Types of games and gamelike activities

Games and activities can last from a few minutes, such as starting games (see page 105), to ten or 15 minutes or longer. Don't try to drag something out just to fill time. Once your child has lost interest, it's a waste of language-learning time. Better to stop earlier and use one or two quick items as fillers.

Many games may already be familiar to your child. She's played them before or watched others playing. Since she knows what to do, she can concentrate on the foreign language used in the game.

Don't be tempted to select games that are too easy and babyish for your child because you think the language level is right. Better to modify the language level of games your child likes and gradually build in new language. Once she knows a lot of the language, begin to repeat and reword it just as you did when she was learning to speak (see page 25).

The first time you play a game or do any type of activity, it most likely won't go as well as you hoped. Don't despair! The second time will be much better.

When you begin, you'll have to do most of the talking. This is natural. Think back to when your child was small. If you use the same prefabricated phrases over and over again for managing games and activities, she'll soon understand and pick them up. In some games she'll soon be capable of switching roles with you and organizing the game and you as well.

Play the same game over and over again. Your child won't find it boring even if you and other adults in your family do. She'll use the opportunity to correct things herself, which is what she wants to do. Self-correction is important in all learning including language learning, and if given the right opportunities, children do it all the time.

Planning

As far as possible, attempt to replicate the same type of conditions as you provided for your child to learn her first language. Although activities will be more sophisticated to match her developmental level, the atmosphere of reassurance and encouragement to use language should be similar.

Don't let the activity dominate. Take into account the language needs and create additional opportunities for interaction. Sometimes pretend not to know something and ask what might be obvious to you. It provides added opportunities for interaction.

"Is it my turn or yours?"   *"Who's next?"*   *"Have I finished?"*
"Is that right?"

Language needs to be planned beforehand to include **management language** for:

- beginning;
- ending;
- sustaining towards the middle when interest may be flagging.

  and **specific language** for the activity or game. This may be new or part new.

Language opportunities need to be built in for:

- interaction;
- understanding one step beyond the present level.

Presentation of the activity or game

This is important, as it sets the scene for everything—mood, enthusiasm, and enjoyment as well as understanding.

Pre-presentation

Introduce all or most of the necessary specific vocabulary in preceding Language Times.

Presentation

- Use management prefabricated phrases for organization, building onto them each time.
- Explain one thing at a time to avoid overloading and the consequent need to translate.
- Control the environment so that you can target the specific language.
- Modify your own language to make understanding easier. Gradually build onto it using parentese techniques.
- Include more repetition than in your normal speech, but without becoming tedious.
- Use the volume of your voice to add suspense and mystery.
- Use slower speech and pauses, without altering the way you say things, in order to keep interest and motivate.
- Create additional opportunities to begin interaction. Ask more questions than you would normally.

Sustaining

This relies heavily on the use of prefabricated phrases for:

- reassurance and encouragement;
- checking progress.

Ending

This provides an opportunity to recall specific language by talking about:

- achievements;
- future plans.

Prefabricated management phrases help to find the winner and tidy up.

Specific language

Simple games and gamelike activities provide a useful base that can be extended and altered to include the specific language needed by your child. The same game or activity can be used for different specific language if the materials are changed.

The game Snap can be used with numbers, things to eat, things to wear, things for transport, or pictures of people doing things, for example, a boy swimming, an elephant eating. Management prefabricated language remains basically the same but is continually expanded. Opportunities for interaction are built in throughout. Your child's nod or one-word reply is reflected back, using parentese techniques, to develop conversation.

Simple activities and games fall into the following basic categories:

Activities

- Physical
- Crafts (coloring, cutting, gluing)
- Drawing

Games

- Physically active games and physical games such as Hide and Seek
- Starting games for finding who will start or be the chaser
- Card games—memory game, Snap, dominoes, Old Maid, Happy Families
- Board games—Lotto, Funny Clowns

Useful management language

For starting an activity

Listen.
Start here.
Copy me.
Have you got the scissors?
Copy me. Cut there.
Paste it.
Stick it here like this.
Draw a . . .
Color this.

For starting a game

Stand here.
Stand in this circle.
Count the cards.
How many have you got?
Put them here.
Give one to you and one to me.
Are you ready? Go.
It's your turn. It's my turn.
Hurry up.

For sustaining an activity

Let's look at it.
That's good.
Try again.
Put some more here.
Show me.

For sustaining a game

Who's next?
That's yours. Is that mine?
How many have you got?
It's your turn again.
Try again.
Show me.

For ending an activity

Have you finished?
Stop now.
Next time we'll do it again.
Put the paste/scissors away.
Put it on the French Table.
That's good. Well done.

For ending a game

Stop. It's time to stop.
Have you finished?
Count your cards/my cards
  please.
How many cards have you/I got?
You're the winner. Well done.
Put the cards away.

Simple games into which specific language can be slotted

Paper, scissors, and rock (international starting game)

In a chorus, say, "one, two, three," or "A, B, C," beating time with your clenched fists. As you say "three" or "C," make one of the following three shapes with your hand:

- clenched fist to represent a rock;
- two straight fingers to represent the blades of a pair of scissors;
- a flat hand to represent a piece of paper.

The decision as to the winner is then made as follows:

- The rock breaks the scissors, so the rock wins.
- The scissors cut the paper, so the scissors win.
- The paper wraps up the rock, so the paper wins.

If you both make the same shape the first time, do it again.

Long and short (a starting game)

Hide a long and a short piece of string or a long and short pencil in the fist of your hand with only the same amount of each showing. Ask your child to say which is longer or shorter. If she guesses right, she wins.

Buzz

Count aloud and instead of saying "three" or a multiple of three, say "Buzz" or the equivalent in the foreign language. If you make a mistake, your child then begins again from zero. The one who counts the furthest without a mistake is the winner.

Simon Says (adapted)

Your child must do whatever Simon says, so if you say, "Simon says, Touch your nose," your child touches her nose. If you say, "Simon says, Don't touch your mouth," and your child disobeys and touches her mouth, she loses one of her five points. Play until she has lost all five points. Choose a foreign language name to replace *Simon*.

Memory game

Make ten pairs of picture cards and place them facedown on a flat surface. Pick up one card and name it—for example "a flower"—and then another and name it. If they match, keep them; if they are different replace them. Play until all the cards have been picked up. The winner has the most cards. This can be extended to practice plurals by saying "two flowers" when the two matching cards are placed together.

Snap

Shuffle ten pairs of picture cards and deal them into two packs. Place a pile in front of each player. Pick up a card and name it— for example "an airplane"—and place it in front of you. Your child then does the same. If two cards are the same shout, "SNAP!" or its equivalent in the foreign language. The player who says "SNAP!" first picks up both piles of turned-up cards, and the game continues. The winner ends up with all the cards. The loser has none. This can be extended to practice plurals by saying, "SNAP! two airplanes."

Lotto (similar to bingo)

Make 18 cards to match the nine spaces on two boards.

The caller keeps the 18 cards and one board. The other player has the second board. The caller shuffles the 18 cards, and puts them in a pile, facedown. The caller then picks up a card and names it. The player who has it shouts, "Me! I've got it!" and names it again. The first player to shout out gets the card and places it on top of the matching space on her board. The winner is the first person to cover all nine spaces on her board.

The monster game (similar to Old Maid)

Shuffle ten pairs of cards plus one extra card with a monster picture. Deal the cards and put any pairs on the table. Then ask, "Have you got a . . . ?" If your child has it, she says, "Yes, I have," and hands over the card. If she hasn't got it, she says, "No, I haven't," and you pick out one of her cards, without looking at them. It's then her turn to ask for something. If you haven't got the card, she picks one of your cards without looking at them. Every time one of you makes a pair, you put it on the table. The loser is the person left with the monster card.

Funny Clowns (similar to Beetle)

His body = 6	His legs = 3
His head = 5	His mouth = 2
His arms = 4	His nose = 2
His eyes = 1	

Throw the dice in turn. You must throw a 6 before you can start; when you do, you can draw the body. Continue throwing the dice and naming the number you have thrown. After saying the number —for example "three"—say the corresponding part of the clown's body, "a leg," then draw it.

The player who completes his clown first and says, "I've finished my Funny Clown," is the winner.

Activities or games for practicing specific language items

Vocabulary

What did you do?

A set of picture cards is placed faceup on the table. Pick up one card, and as you show it say, "I went to the supermarket and I bought a . . . " Your child then picks up a card and says, "I went to the supermarket and I bought . . . " repeating the first card and adding her card. The game continues until all the cards have been picked up. If someone makes a mistake, begin the game again.

The same game can be adapted—for example, to "I packed my suitcase and I put in . . . " (to practice items of clothing) or "I went to the beach and I saw a . . . " (to teach vocabulary ready for a beach holiday).

Numbers

Introduce numbers in the following stages: 1–5, 5–10, 10s to 100, 10–20, 21–30.

Games
- Stand-on
- Lotto
- Snap
- Memory game—add together the two matching cards (3 and 3 make 6)

Nouns with indefinite article a/an
Game
- Lotto

Activity
Cutting and pasting pictures of things from magazines (a car, a bicycle, a plane)

Plurals of nouns
Game
- Memory game: name the cards, put a pair together, and say "two . . ."

Commands
Games
- Stand-on (adapted), page 81
- Simon Says (adapted), page 98

Parts of the face
Activities
- Make a puppet face and fasten it onto a stick.
- Decorate a balloon as a face.

Parts of the body
Games
- Funny Clowns
- Simon Says

Clothes
Games
- Lotto
- I packed my suitcase and I put in a . . .

Activities
- Cutting from a clothes catalog to make a picture.
- Get dressed or undressed while talking about it.

Prepositions
Game
- Hide and Seek

Activity
- Make comic strip about a lost animal by cutting trees, flowers, etc., from magazines.

Names of rooms
Activity
- Cut pictures from magazines.

Verbs (present continuous)
Game
- Memory game. Use cards with pictures of people doing things—for example, a woman driving a car or a boy riding a bicycle.

Verb (simple past)

Game

What did you see?	Picture Dictation
What did you do?	I went on a magic carpet and I saw a man. He had three eyes, four ears, etc.

Feelings

Activity

- Make faces for *I'm happy, I'm sad, I'm cross, He's laughing, She's crying.*
- Cook face biscuits (see page 144).

"Can I have . . . ?"

Activity

- Cut from catalogs things that you want to buy.

"I like" and "I don't like"

Activity

- Cut things out from a catalog, such as foods that you like and don't like.

Developing listening skills

Listening is the basis of all language skills. It involves more than hearing (see page 26) and is a skill that can be developed through experience. A child who plays a musical instrument has learned to listen and generally picks up a foreign language quickly once she's aware of what is expected of her. Expectation contributes to good listening, so give your child some guidelines as to what she should listen for.

If you think your child is not a good listener, you can help her to begin in your own language. Begin by being silent and listening for half a minute. Can she hear an airplane? What else did she hear? Compare notes. Did you both hear the same?

Using games and activities to evaluate progress in listening

Stand-on game (page 89), Simon Says (page 106)
- Vary the activities so that your child can't predict and has to listen carefully.
- Reduce gesture and body-language clues to a minimum so that she has to depend on listening correctly.

Picture or number dictation
Have quick sessions lasting only a few minutes. Here is an example:

> *"Draw a tree. Put seven apples in the tree. Two apples are yellow, four apples are red, and one is green. There's a blackbird near the green apple, etc."*

Audiocassette recordings and videos of rhymes, songs, or stories

Initially, listening sessions should be short. Ask your child to listen for something specific. Play back so that she can listen a second time to check. Build up gradually until she can listen to a complete recording.

Rhymes, rhyme games, chants, and finger play rhymes

If you feel worried and shy about your ability in the foreign language, it is possible to help your child a lot by just using rhymes and chants. You can back up your spoken language by a cassette recording. You can extend the rhymes and chants your child learns by linked crafts and drawing activities. As long as you select simple rhymes, plan how you're going to introduce them, and extend them through activities, you'll be able to help your child to understand and use some foreign language. You'll also give her confidence and self-esteem, both of which are important in language learning. Rhymes and chants provide an easily learned foundation in the foreign language. Their value in language learning is both underestimated and underutilized.

Children pick up rhymes and chants quickly and in much the same way as they do in their own language. They seem to enjoy reciting them aloud and especially to appreciative adult audiences.

> *A boy, aged six, said after saying two rhymes very fast, "Now I can say a lot of German, just like grown-ups when they talk."*

To a child, rhymes and chants are prefabricated phrases. Second verses into which new words have been slotted are partially prefabricated phrases (see page 30). If a child hears short rhymes or chants several times, he picks them up.

Selection

Rhymes need to be carefully selected for their language as well as interest content. They need to sound attractive, too. In selecting rhymes:

- check to see if the language is useful to your child;
- check if the language can be transferred to other situations.

Although traditional rhymes have their place, most, because of their language content, are better left until later when your child can already use quite a lot of language.

It's possible to alter or make up your own simple rhymes or chants to fit in with your child's needs. This action rhyme was personalized, the child's own name, Tommy Jones, being substituted for Teddy Bear.

> *Tommy Jones, Tommy Jones*
> *Turn around,*
> *Tommy Jones, Tommy Jones*

Touch the ground
Tommy Jones, Tommy Jones
Show your shoes,
Tommy Jones, Tommy Jones
Tell your news.

and he tells
I went to . . .
I'm happy

Chants can also be adapted or made up on the spot:

Cold, cold, much too cold.
Hot, hot, it's not hot. (pretending to lick an ice cream cone)

or to fit the rhythm of a train going faster and faster along the track:

Pears and plums, pears and plums,
Apples and oranges, apples and oranges,
Pineapples and figs,
FRUIT.

Follow this up by making a fruit salad and eating it.

Cassettes, videos, CD-ROMs, CDs

Material is available in various formats that you can use to back up your voice, once you have presented the rhyme or chant. If you can't obtain a suitable recording, write out your own collection and ask a foreign friend to record a cassette for you.

New CD-ROM and CD materials are published each year. Find out what may be useful to you and your child.

Presentation of rhymes, chants, and finger plays

You may feel better if you introduce some of the specific rhyme language before you introduce the rhyme, but it is not absolutely necessary, as your child can pick up the language as one phrase, for example, "Touch-the-ground."

You may find it necessary to tell her what the rhyme is about in your own language, but don't be tempted to give her a word-for-word translation.

Show her instead by mime, in a picture, or use a concrete object. Understanding a rhyme is easier than understanding isolated phrases, as rhymes represent a complete item or story (as, for example, the Tommy Jones rhyme does).

Step-by-step presentation

Step 1

Say the rhyme yourself and ask your child to listen. It's easier to start with an action rhyme. The actions help understanding. The rhythm and rhyming language are attractive.

Explain the meaning and isolate specific words, supporting them with a picture or an action to help understanding.

Repeat it a second time, getting her to join in the actions.

Repeat it a third time, getting her to join in again.

Repeat it a fourth time and go on to another activity.

Repeat it once again before you end the session or at some appropriate time later in the day before your child goes to bed. Repetition after some delay helps in learning.

Step 2

The second time you present the rhyme, ask your child to join in. She'll probably do so without too much difficulty.

Repeat it again together. She'll do it even better.

The third time, leave off the ending of some lines without making any comment and see if she'll complete them by herself. If she has difficulty, help her by using a softer and encouraging voice.

Repeat it a fourth time in the same way and then change to another activity.

Before you end the session, say the rhyme together once again. Find some time before bedtime to say it together once more.

Step 3

The third time you present the rhyme, say it together and then ask your child to say it. You'll probably have to help, especially with small words such as *and*, *the*, and *in*. Let her try again. It'll be much better. If she seems interested, let her say it a third time by herself and just join in the actions. She is now ready to listen to the recording. Let her listen and she'll gradually adjust her pronunciation until it matches the speaker on the recording. Once she has got to this stage, unless you are confident about your pronunciation, start off a rhyme, but let her voice dominate as her pronunciation may be closer to the recording.

Once she can say the rhyme really well, make sure you give her a chance to show it off to the rest of the family. Their praise will motivate her to go on learning more rhymes.

Many parents find that they can introduce a new rhyme, chant, or finger play each week. Like this they gradually build up a repertoire from which they can select material for sing-along or other informal Quickies with the family.

Rhyme games

Starting (selecting) games

Most languages are rich in starting rhyme games that eliminate players by counting or other means in order to select a leader or a chaser (see page 103).

Some of these games have become international (see page 105), and it is fun to play them in a different language.

Apple, peach, pear, apricot	*Pomme, pêche, poire, abricot.*
There is one	*Y en a une*
There is one	*Y en a une*
There is one	*Y en a une*
Too many.	*De trop.*

Other rhyme games exist that are not starting games (for example, "Round and round the garden goes the little mouse"). It's possible to add your own gamelike activity to some rhymes. This gives you the opportunity to introduce game management language ("It's your turn," etc., see page 104).

Linked activities

Rhymes and chants can provide the content base from which you can develop crafts, cooking, and drawing and painting activities, such as making a fruit salad or collecting the names of ice cream flavors in German. Activities provide opportunities to practice the rhyme or chant language in everyday situations.

Learning to read through rhymes

Through rhymes and chants your child will be introduced effortlessly to the sounds and ways of saying the language. She will build up a bank of expressions and words that she knows how to pronounce correctly. She will begin to use the rhymes as reference, going back to them when she wants to know how to say a word. It is interesting that adults who have forgotten how to speak a foreign language can still say rhymes they learned in childhood.

It is well known that children who have had a lot of experience with rhyming sounds learn to read more easily. In any language a child finds learning to read easier if she starts by reading rhymes she can already say from memory.

In a foreign language, learning to read through rhymes is an excellent way to begin, as it assures that children read with the right pronunciation. Once they know many rhymes and chants by memory, they can start reading, providing they already read in their own language (see page 125). Older children want to read, and if you delay it too long, they can be frustrated. Before you introduce reading, make sure your child knows the alphabet in the foreign language and can name all the letters (see page 123).

Making rhyme cards and books

Once children can read rhymes they already know by heart, they enjoy copying them to make birthday cards or onto individual sheets to be put together to make their own rhyme books. Personalizing the rhyme collection by making your own book is important—it's different from a published collection of rhymes. Grown children are still known to keep on their bookshelves the German Rhyme Book made when they were little.

Songs

Songs also play an important role in language learning, but it should be borne in mind that some songs distort pronunciation to fit the music. Children also have difficulty in transferring sung language to spoken language. To help them over this, it's a good idea to say the words of a song rather than sing it.

Some children's songs in a foreign language have too great a vocabulary load for beginners and so are best left until later. Others are too musically complex. Select songs that have an easy-to-copy rhythm, are repetitive, and to which you can add actions if they haven't already got them. Add a refrain, too, if there isn't one by repeating the last line or lines.

Remember, you don't have to be an excellent singer to present songs to your child. Once children know the song, they soon improve the way they sing it until it more or less matches the recording. In selecting a recording, don't choose one made by a professional opera singer, as his or her voice will be too far removed from the way you or your child sings and you won't be able to copy it.

Presentation of a song

Play the recording before Warm-up on several occasions before you actually present the song. In this way your child will already be familiar with it.

Step 1

- First tell your child what the song is about, using actions, a picture, or some concrete object to help understanding. Then sing part of the song to her.
- Repeat the same part of the song.
- Say the words.
- Sing it once again and ask her if she would like to clap while you sing. She may even try to join in singing.
- Repeat it again so that she has a chance to do it better and then change the activity.
- Just before you finish Language Time or before she goes to bed, sing it again and let her join in the actions. Some parents say bath time is a good time for singing together!

Step 2

- First sing the familiar part of the song and let her clap and join in.
- Then present the rest of the song and repeat it.
- Say the new lines.
- Sing it all again asking her to clap and join in if she wants. Repeat it again so that she has a chance to improve her performance.
- Now listen to the recording together. She may not be able to join in at this stage but will be able to understand the recording.

Step 3

- Sing the song together.
- Repeat it.

- Then sing the song with the recording.
- Then sing the song taking turns line by line. Start it off yourself. Repeat it. It'll be better the second time.

Recordings

Use recordings as much as possible once you have introduced the song yourself. If you can't get the type of recording you need, ask a friend to make one for you.

Sing-alongs

Try building up a repertoire for sing-alongs. Sing-alongs are a good method of warming up. They're also useful informal Quickies on a car journey, at a family gathering, or at bath time.

You need to keep up the momentum in sing-along programs. Items can include rhymes and chants, reciting games as well as songs. Don't always select the program yourself. Ask your child to make her own program. When you're out with the family, let everyone have a choice.

Vary the way you sing or say items. Take it in turns, verse by verse, line by line. Alter the volume of your voice and the speed. Sing-alongs can be great fun, and you'll find with practice you'll improve.

Questions parents ask

"My son doesn't seem to pick up rhymes very quickly."

Have you checked his hearing ability? He may be managing in his own language by an increased use of lip reading. He can't do this in the foreign language when he's just beginning to learn. Stand behind him and say something in your own language and see if he responds. Then say something in the foreign language, removing all the clues to understanding including body language. Does he understand? If you are in doubt, take him for a medical checkup.

Children have difficulty in hearing when they have a cold. This is only temporary. If your child has a cold, make sure that you repeat things often enough and in a way he can hear and also lip read. If you introduce new language too quickly when he has difficulty in hearing, he won't understand.

> "My daughter is getting her new front teeth and finds it difficult to say some things. Should I make her repeat them?"

Losing front teeth is a difficult time for your child, and until she has grown her new front ones, the way she says some sounds is bound to be different. Say things together, but don't ask her to say anything by herself until she feels comfortable with her new teeth. She will be learning and having fun in spite of her teeth. Don't embarrass her by making her say something she can't say because of the gap at the front of her mouth. Any embarrassment could put her off language learning for life. The same advice applies to children who have dental braces on their teeth for short periods. Once the braces are removed, the child needs time to adjust the way she makes sounds to fit the different shape of her mouth cavity.

Final thoughts

Parents who like a foreign language can enjoy playing games or reciting rhymes. Through them they can pass on enjoyment and enthusiasm to their children, and at the same time give them a useful foundation in the language. Personalization and transmission of enthusiasm and enjoyment are vital components of the learning process. This is especially true in the case of young children.

CHAPTER SEVEN

Reading and Writing

Most children who can already read in their own language take learning to read a foreign language in their stride, providing they can speak a certain amount and know something about the sound system. They've usually picked up a lot of information on sounds from rhymes and chants. Children who can already read know about the purpose and mechanics of reading and have only to work out how to decode the written foreign language. If they begin by reading language that they can already speak, decoding is much easier, and they get the pronunciation right. Children like working out how to decode foreign-language text. They find it an interesting challenge. It's like cracking a magic or secret code, which fascinates many children at the age of eight or nine.

Timing the introduction of reading

Children need to be able to speak some foreign language before they begin to read. This is what they did in their own language. However, don't make your child wait too long before you let him read as you may demotivate him. Two years is a long time to wait if you can already read in your own language. If you're going to visit the country, you'll be surrounded by written advertisements, notices, and other text when you get there, and he'll want to read them. If he can't read anything, he'll be disappointed, and if he tries, he'll read them as he reads his own language, and the pronunciation will be all wrong.

If you write in a different script from the foreign language, don't worry; your child will soon learn the new writing script. Introduce writing gradually and begin by making the shapes by arm movements in the air. If you can get hold of some sandpaper letters or script shapes, you'll find your child learns even more quickly, as touch, using the index and middle fingers, adds to what is learned in the arm movements. Remember, fingers that have just been washed are more sensitive to touch.

If your child asks if he can read, let him start by reading rhymes he can already say by heart. Reading rhymes will probably satisfy his initial desire and curiosity. It will also enable you to delay the introduction of other reading material until later, when he is capable of using more language.

If your child doesn't know how to read, it's better to help him develop his skills in his own language and delay introducing reading in a foreign language.

Introducing the alphabet

Before you introduce reading, you'll need to introduce the names of the letters of the alphabet, otherwise the child will have to use his own alphabet letter names to talk about the words in the foreign language. Apart from being unnatural, it interferes with learning. Obviously, if the writing script is different, he has to learn the new writing script before you start reading. The quickest way is to use the foreign-language alphabet song. Alphabet songs are hard to find but do exist. People who learned a foreign language as adults usually don't know them. If you can't find a recording, ask a foreign-language-speaking parent.

Step 1

Sing the alphabet song and repeat it as far as the letter *g*.

If you can't find a cassette recording of the song, ask a native speaker to make a recording for you.

Step 2

Sing the alphabet as far as *g* and introduce the letters up to *n*.

Step 3

Sing the alphabet as far as *n* and introduce the letters up to *t*.

Step 4

Sing the alphabet as far as *t* and introduce the letters up to *z*.

Once your child knows the letter names, introduce letter cards and discuss the similarities and differences. Talk about accents and different letter shapes, if there are any. At this stage it's better not to introduce the different styles in handwriting used in foreign languages, as they may be very different from the style he uses at school—for example, German cursive handwritten shapes are often difficult for adults to decipher. Later on, when he can read quite well, he'll enjoy trying to decode handwriting. In the early stages, different handwriting styles may provide an extra learning challenge.

Most people, even in their own language, find it difficult to say the sounds of the letters in isolation. It's much easier when vowel letters are linked to consonants. The sounds of some languages are easier to remember than others, and unless you are very sure of the sounds, it's better not to use individual letter sounds. Help your child to listen to sounds within words he already knows and help him to recognize rhyming words. You can help him to learn a great deal about sounds from language he already knows and can use. At the same time you'll be helping him to develop his listening skills.

The following games also help in recognizing sounds:

I-Spy game

This helps your child to recognize initial sounds. Say, "I can see something beginning with *b*" (making the letter sound as it does in the word, that is, not "bee" but "b—") and hold up the letter card. Then add, "What is it?" looking in the direction of the thing. Your child has to guess. Emphasize the first letter sound several times together, before asking again.

Rhyming game

This is a gamelike activity that plays with rhyming words or sounds. Say a rhyme and then select one of the rhyming words from it. Ask your child to tell you some of the other words that rhyme with it. Some children are great at playing with their own language and can transfer these skills—once they have been shown how—to a foreign language. If your child finds it difficult in the foreign language, practice together at a different time in your own language.

Reading through rhymes and chants

Once your child knows about 15 rhymes or chants well and has practiced the language on different occasions, providing he can already read, you can begin reading in the foreign language.

Make your own book of rhymes and chants by handwriting or printing them. Put one rhyme on each double spread so that each rhyme represents a single experience for your child. Write in bold script, leaving a good space between verses. Photocopy or print a second copy of each rhyme and keep them as single sheets.

Step 1

Start by the simplest chant or rhyme. If it involves more than about eight words, only introduce half the words to begin with.

Make flash cards of the words and introduce them one by one. Then show your child how to write the rhyme by putting the flash cards down in lines to resemble the printed text as you say the words. Repeat, letting him "write" the rhyme as you say it.

One	two	three
Jump	with	me
Jump	jump	jump
Jump	like	me

This rhyme has a total of eight words. *One, two, three* were already known, so there were five new words.

Step 2

Repeat step 1. If you have not completed the rhyme, finish it. If you have already completed it, introduce flash cards for a new rhyme. Then write it using the flash cards. Don't introduce too many flash cards at a time.

Once your child can write three or four rhymes in this way, show him the sheet of the first rhyme. He'll find he can read it. Don't forget to praise him. Let him decorate the page and read it several times together. Keep the decorated sheet in a folder.

Continue introducing flash cards for rhymes in the same way. Don't introduce the text sheets at the same time as you write the rhyme with flash cards. There should always be a delay between the two activities.

When your child has completed all the sheets, let him put them together to make his own rhyme book. Put your copy of the rhyme book with the other books in the Language Corner.

Games for reading

Once your child can read some rhymes, extend his reading to games he has already played with pictures. As with rhymes he can already use the specific language of these games and so will read with the correct pronunciation.

Memory game

Change one of the pictures of each pair of cards to writing. It is important not to write just the noun *dog* but to include the indefinite article *a dog*. Gender of nouns (masculine, feminine, or neuter) is learned through practice. With practice it gradually becomes automatic. Introduce a few written cards at a time until all the pairs consist of one picture and one written card.

Snap

Alter the words as in the memory game.

Lotto

Alter all the spaces on the boards to show writing.

Introduce new games and gamelike activities for reading practice. For example, make treasure hunt clue cards showing "under the table" or "on the big chair."

Reading books

Story books

Spoken language is different from written language. Many children find it difficult in their own language to make the bridge between spoken or conversational language and the more formal style of written language. For this reason it's best to begin with foreign language books written in a spoken style of language, as this is the type of language your child knows and uses. Later, when he has more experience, introduce books with a written style of language.

Begin with storybooks that he already knows—you've already told him the story by showing him the pictures but without reading the text. If you've told the story several times, he probably already knows some of the language by heart, which will help him in decoding.

Step 1

Introduce some of the words by flash cards. These might be the words on the front cover. Talk about the sounds of the first letters and let him match the flash cards with the words. Then take a flash card and see if you can find the same word on other pages in the book.

Step 2

Repeat step 1 and introduce flash cards for the first page of the story. The text should be only one or, at the most, two sentences. Let him write the text with the flash cards.

Continue page by page in the same way until he can read the whole book. Words will repeat themselves, so you will find you need to make fewer flash cards as you get further into the story. He'll also get better and quicker at reading as he gets more practice.

Continue introducing many very simple books until he builds up his own library of simple books he can read. As he increases his personal bank of words, talk to him about words. Point out for example that some letters at the end of words are silent; he doesn't say them. Ask him if he can find some more words like this. Showing him how to look at words helps him to work out spelling rules for himself. If you tell him the rules, he isn't likely to remember them.

Foreign-language, picture storybooks

It is worth making a collection of books that are originally written and illustrated in the foreign language, as from them he'll be able to absorb some foreign culture and gain an insight into a different way of life. It is valuable for your child to know some stories belonging to the foreign culture, as it will help him to fit into society more easily if the occasion arises.

"International" picture storybooks

These are books that have been translated into many different languages, like the Spot series, Babar books, Tintin, Asterix, etc. Although the text is in a different language, the content of the text and illustrations represents the culture in which the story was originally written. Where the text is simple and in a spoken-style language, your child might enjoy reading some of them. If he has already read them in his own language, he knows the story, which means he only needs to decode the text.

Translating favorite books

Some parents translate their children's favorite story books into the foreign language. They handwrite the text under the printed text themselves. In some cases they ask for help in translation from foreign-language friends and ask them at the same time to record a cassette.

Picture books and cassettes

Cassettes can be a useful back-up once you have presented a story yourself. The way you present a story is important. Without your personal presentation your child will take much longer before he understands and enjoys the story. By personalizing the story, you make it more easily accessible for your child.

Children enjoy listening to recordings, especially if they are well made with good sound effects. When your child knows the story well, he can listen to the recording without following it in the book. If the story includes a lot of dialogue, you'll soon find that he knows it all by heart. This can lead to making a puppet play or acting the story.

Bilingual picture dictionaries

Children enjoy looking at bilingual picture dictionaries and finding words they can read in two languages. If your child already knows both words well, you'll be amazed how he reads each word with perfect pronunciation. If he doesn't know how to read the foreign word, he may try to decode it using the sounds of his own language. The result will be that he says it using his own language pronunciation. Don't comment on this; just repeat it correctly.

Bilingual picture dictionaries provide a source of translated words, but may not always provide the correct pictorial information. For example, bread differs in appearance from culture to culture. For this reason it's a good idea to try and buy a monolingual picture dictionary published in the foreign language, instead of a monolingual dictionary to which a second language has been added to make it bilingual. The pictures in the monolingual dictionary will be culturally correct. The selection of monolingual picture dictionaries is generally better in the country of origin, so try and look for one when you go abroad.

However, whatever picture dictionary you use, you can have fun and at the same time help your child to develop skills in using a dictionary. He'll also get extra practice in using articles (*a* and *the*).

Ask your child to "Find a . . . " in the dictionary. Make it into a game by adding some suspense to your voice.

Point to something and ask him, "What's this in Spanish?"

Ask him to show you his favorite animal, his favorite toy, etc.

After using published bilingual dictionaries, you may like to make your own picture dictionary in the foreign language (see page 142).

CD-ROMs and CDs

If your child is used to working with these in his own language, try and get him a suitable disk in the foreign language. He'll teach himself a lot, but the information will be passive. He won't be able to transfer it to the spoken form unless you help him. Try and work together sometimes. Talk about the illustrations on the screen and transfer some of the language to your daily life.

Textbooks

Use a textbook as a guide for yourself, but don't show it to your child. Although good textbooks may include some useful activities, the use of one might spoil your special atmosphere. It could make your child feel that you were teaching him and that learning a language is like being at school. This could alter his attitude to learning and to you.

Handwriting

Children's handwriting styles differ from country to country. It is not necessary for your child to change his style of handwriting when he writes to match the style of the foreign language.

If he makes any comment about the different style, ask him what differences he notices. He may find it difficult to decode some of the handwritten styles. Don't worry: many adults do as well. Help him to read what is necessary and don't waste too much time on it at this stage.

Copying

Copying is very important and often underestimated. Spelling is partly learned through the motor skills of writing words. So give your child plenty of opportunity to copy things, but make sure that there's some real purpose for making the copy. For example, rhymes for a book, a list for shopping, for messages, for invitations.

Creative writing

Until your child has plenty of experience, creative writing is best done as a cooperative effort. If your child writes a postcard to a pen pal, compose the text together in spoken language. Then write the text down for him to copy. He can dictate it to you and watch you write it word by word. He'll learn more from copying the correct text than trying to write words which he doesn't know how to spell and gets wrong because he hasn't had sufficient experience in the language.

Grammar

Children find out by themselves how language works. They've done it successfully in their own language and can do it in the foreign language, if we let them and give them sufficient opportunities to build up their own awareness of the language patterns. This preparatory period is essential. Don't fall into the trap of trying to tell them the rules of grammar. It won't make learning any quicker. In any case they may not understand the way you explain the rules, as it isn't necessarily the way they see the language.

The best contribution to grammar learning you can make is to help your child develop his awareness of the patterns of the language. You can do this by targeting specific language groups. For example, in French, you can play the memory game one day using all masculine words and the next time using all feminine words. He might comment on this. If he doesn't, you can draw his attention to it. Wait and see what he says about it. Don't be tempted immediately to give him an adult rule. Gender is best learned through use and in time you develop a feel for it. You might have a laugh about gender though, as there are some surprises—for example, in French, *un soldat* (a soldier) but *une sentinelle* (a sentry or guard).

As he did in his own language, he will gradually use information that he has stored as a point of reference when coping with new language. Of course, he won't always get it right, because he may be applying a general rule to an exception (see page 27), but carry on dealing with mistakes by repeating the language correctly. Boys tend to be more worried about making mistakes in a foreign language than girls. They don't want to be seen as stupid and so won't take a risk. It's important to encourage your child to take risks as this is one of the ways he learns.

If he's already learning grammar in his own language, he might try to transfer his information to the foreign language. Help him collect nouns and verbs, if this is what he wants to do.

If a foreign language is a subject at school and he is being taught formal grammar rules, you can help him by giving him as much experience as you can using items of language involving these rules. Don't confuse him by attempting to reteach the rules. You may not do it in exactly the same way as the teacher. It is important to support the way he works and not supplant it by introducing rules in the way you see them.

Spelling

Your child already knows about the mechanics of spelling in his own language and will transfer some of his learning skills to the foreign language. Try to get your child used to spelling using the letter names of the foreign language alphabet, for example, the letter y in French is called *e grec*. Until he can do this, progress will be limited, as he will be continually switching back into his own language. Sometimes ask him to spell words aloud when he's copying words from a text. However, don't spell them letter by letter. Try and break them into syllables so that he gets used to groups of letters that often go together, such as *do-ing* and *care-ful*.

Collect acronyms used in the foreign language. For example, SNCF and TGV in French railway timetables.

Don't try and make him learn spelling by heart. Words learned out of context in this way are soon forgotten.

Instead, help him to look at words by:

- making comments about the letters, patterns, accents, and shapes;
- playing with rhyming words;
- breaking words into syllables (*do-ing*, *play-ing*, *e-le-phant*, *te-le-vision*);
- collecting prefixes and suffixes;
- looking at initial and final letters, pairs, or groups of letters.

Help him to listen to words and how they change. Even young children can hear the change in sound of adjectives to agree with feminine words—for example, in French *vert/verte* (meaning "green," masculine/feminine), *petit/petite* ("small," masculine/feminine). They don't need to be taught the rules of agreement on which many adults are dependent.

Enjoy words with your child. By doing this he'll develop an interest in them and be confident about what they mean and how to use them. The greater his experience with words, the more likely he is to spell them correctly.

Questions parents ask

"My son is nine and reads German with an English accent. What can I do?"

He does this because he started reading before he had sufficient experience in speaking German. He is using the techniques he uses for decoding English in decoding German, so he reads the words as English words. Don't let him read any German that he can't already speak. Learn some rhymes and chants together and then let him read them (see page 125). Then move on to playing reading games (see page 127). In this way he'll build up a bank of words he can read. At the same time he will be working out the sound system and how sounds relate to letters. Then introduce him to stories, but tell the story several times beforehand so that he knows the language before he begins reading. By now he'll be starting to read using German decoding techniques which he has gradually worked out through experience.

> "My son wants to know what every word means when he reads Spanish."

Boys are more worried about making mistakes than girls, and this may be part of the problem. Maybe the texts are too difficult. Build up his confidence by giving him plenty of experience in rhymes, songs, and easy texts. Talk about words with him (see page 134) and make sure that he's already encountered any new words in a text and reduce his stress in this way. Make a dictionary with him and teach him how to use a printed dictionary so that he can look up words himself. These varied experiences will help him alter his approach to texts.

Final thoughts

The richer the experience the quicker the child will work out the systems of the language and construct his own grammar. Parents are in a position to provide their children with rich experiences. Working on a one-to-one basis, they can give them individual attention—activities don't have to be shared with the rest of a class. To speed up learning, parents can help children develop their awareness of the sounds of the language as well as the underlying structures. These varied experiences in the foreign language will be reflected in children's insights into their own language.

CHAPTER EIGHT

Stories, projects, and other learning opportunities

Stories

The importance of stories to your child for her all-around well-being and development, and especially creative and language development, should not be underestimated. Young children utter almost all they say through real or invented stories, in many different ways. They also learn what other people say and think through stories. Adults make use of story more than they suppose. Think back to the conversation at your last family meal or the last telephone conversation you had with a friend. It probably included one or two stories about what had happened and maybe some description of future plans, too.

It is well known that the frequency with which a child is read to in her own language greatly influences her later success at school. The same is true for a foreign language. However, it's not just the reading that's important, it's the selection of the story and the interaction of talk that goes on before, during, and after a story. You know for yourself that having seen a good film, the story keeps coming back again and again in your mind, and you enjoy talking it over with someone else who's seen it. It's the same for your child. So make sure that you read the same story again and that you come back to it after some time. Refer to it in informal Shorties, too. Repetition is important for language learning, and some of the story language may become in-family language.

A Mexican boy, aged eight, having read and acted the story Red Hen's Cake, *finally made the cake with his mother. By this time he knew most of the language by heart. One day his mother asked him, in his own language, if he could help her with some housework. He replied with the English used in* Red Hen's Cake, *"Sorry, I can't. I'm busy." After this, whenever his mother needed help, she asked, "Can you help me, please?" and the reply, positive or negative, was always in the English from the story. Soon it became the family habit for any member of the family to reply in English. The habit lasted for many years.*

Using stories

Long before your child begins reading in the foreign language, you can introduce stories.

Make up your own short stories based on:

- pictures you draw;
- a toy or "the foreign friend" (see page 58);
- a puppet;
- the pictures in a picture story book;
- a picture or pictures in an advertisement in a foreign-language magazine.

Stories about the "friend" can develop into a mini-soap opera. Each Language Time, recount a new episode in his daily life saga. Most children are used to the soap opera style of storytelling, and since it recounts familiar actions, it provides an additional interesting and personalized language opportunity.

A picture story

Step 1

Divide a piece of paper into six squares and number them. Cut out six pieces of furniture from a foreign-language catalog or magazine. Stick one piece of furniture onto each square. Cut out a small butterfly, a bee, or a fly and place it in the first picture—perhaps on the sofa.

Ask your child, "Where's the fly?" She replies, "It's on the sofa." or "on the sofa." Continue: "Where's the fly now?" placing the fly on a picture of a chair. Continue until you've finished the six pictures.

Step 2

The second time, let the child put the fly where she wants and ask you the questions.

Step 3

The third time, let her draw the fly in the pictures and you ask the questions. Let her make a seventh picture on the other side of one of the pieces of paper of the fly flying away into the sky. Say together, "Bye, bye fly."

Similar stories can be made up about:

- cars in a town;
- an animal—a pet, a dinosaur;
- a child in a store;
- a journey using pictures from a ferry catalog;
- a visit to a city such as Paris ("by the Eiffel Tower" "up the Eiffel Tower").

Stories transfer easily to playing Hide-and-Seek–type games (see page 95).

Published story picture books (see page 128)

Before you introduce a story, read the story yourself several times and work out the essential story line and language. Decide what points in the story are essential for understanding and what language you want your child to remember and begin to use. A good way to work this out is to imagine that you are rewriting the story as a short script for acting. You may find that you have to leave out some episodes and a great deal of detail the first few times you tell the story. Don't worry about this. Gradually expand the story over several readings until your child can manage the complete story.

Practice telling or reading the story beforehand in a spare moment. Some people find it useful to practice in front of a mirror. A run-through gives you an opportunity to try out using your foreign language and see how well you can combine it with:

- speaking or reading slowly and clearly without distortion;
- including pauses to add excitement;
- using high, low, soft, loud, and gruff voices where necessary;
- using your eyes well;
- using the pictures appropriately.

Find some way of presenting the story to your child. Lead into it by reminding her in her own language, if necessary, of something similar she did or you did together. "Do you remember when . . . ?"

Encourage her to join in refrains or actually say some of the spoken language by herself, if she can, just as she did when you read her stories when she was little. She'll love using a deep voice for the giant or adding the meows for the cat. Give her time to look at the pictures and reflect.

Once you've introduced the entire story, she's ready to look at the book and listen to the cassette at the same time. You'll soon find that she knows most of it by heart. Then she'll want to read it to you. You might start by sharing, each reading a page to take some of the load off her. But be warned: She'll probably make some comment about your pronunciation not being like the cassette.

Drama

Stories naturally lead to acting. Since there are only two of you, it's probably best to do simple puppet plays in which you both take part. It's not necessary to spend a lot of time making complicated puppets. The effect for the child seems to be about the same whatever the shape or size of the puppet; the main aim is to use the puppet as a language experience.

Simple puppets can be cardboard, made by drawing the shape of the character from the hips upwards and making two holes in the stomach. The index and middle fingers fit into the holes and act as legs so the puppets can walk. Making the puppets provides a wonderful opportunity to talk about parts of the body.

The stage can be something quite simple such as the edge of a table or the back of a chair. The child hides behind the tablecloth or the chair to manipulate the puppets. For children a simple show like this is effective and satisfying. As the main aim is foreign-language learning, it's better to produce more plays than spend the time making a complicated stage that doesn't provide a richer language experience.

You may find that you have to rewrite the story in spoken form for your play. If you do, write it clearly and photocopy it, so that your child can read the text. She should be able to read it correctly and with good pronunciation, as she already knows most of the language by heart. Don't forget to include the stage directions; it's useful language and makes the script more fun and accurate. After you've acted out the play, put a copy of the script on the bookshelf in the Language Corner. Your child and other members of the family might like to read it.

Before you put on your show, record it, and play back. It's an interesting and useful activity. Your child will point out all the mistakes she's made, and yours as well. Let her have an opportunity to get them right. Record it a second time and see how it's improved. You'll be amazed by her ability to self-correct. Make an additional copy of the cassette and put it with the script in the Language Corner.

Send invitations and make some programs and tickets, too. This will lead naturally to talking about time and days of the week. Copying gives good practice in getting to know how words are written in the foreign language. It also helps in learning to spell (see page 133).

By now your child knows the characters in the play quite well, so suggest to her that she could write her own story about them. She may pick up the idea, but if she doesn't, never mind. She may not be ready yet. If she shows interest, explain to her how to use speech bubbles for the spoken language: it saves time and is much easier. You may find you have to help her a little and that the finished product is a joint venture. Don't worry about this. She will have learned a lot from it, like an apprentice, and next time maybe she'll suggest doing a story and do most of it by herself.

It's wiser to leave role-play activities—such as going shopping in a foreign culture—until your child has had first-hand experience or a good second-hand experience through a picture book and cassette or video. Role-play involves acting out another culture. If you ask her to play the role of a German shopkeeper before she has had the chance to experience German culture, she will be acting the role of the German using her own cultural resources, because she knows no other. This can be very confusing for the child, as culture and language are intertwined, and in the German situation, shop culture is different from that in the U.S. In fact, an experience of role play before your child has experience of the German way of life can be counterproductive. It may serve to reinforce her imaginary ideas of what it's like to be a German. Once in place, these ideas may be difficult to erase and could hinder her natural ability to absorb another culture. It may also contribute to culture shock when she finds that reality doesn't match the image she has created in the role-play. Of course, if you are role-playing animals it's different, as a white duck is a duck in any language, though his "quack quack" is not imitated in the same way in different languages.

A picture dictionary

Making a picture dictionary:

- introduces dictionary skills by showing the relationship between letters and the sounds of the foreign language;
- provides a personalized source of reference for spelling.

Using a plain notebook, help your child write the capital and small letter for each alphabet letter at the top of a double-spread page. It may take two Language Times to complete the alphabet. Progress is greatly helped by singing the Alphabet Song (see pages 123–124) to remind your child of the letter sequence. Extra pages can be left for information such as letters with accents and groups of words such as colors and numbers.

Collect pictures from foreign-language magazines so that the cultural content is correct. Advertisements given out at supermarket checkouts show everyday things such as milk in the right-shaped carton and sandwiches made with different bread. Getting the right visual image helps children to build up their concepts of the foreign culture. Give your child a picture and tell her how to say it in the foreign language. Say it together and then ask her to find the appropriate page to enter the picture. Then let her copy the word. Include the indefinite article (*a/an* in English) with nouns, as this gives added practice in the use of gender. Include verbs in the infinitive form (*to run* in English). Your child will be using several verb tenses and this will give you a chance to talk about them and how they change—for example, *go* becomes *went* in the past tense. Later on, you can make some special "verb pages" at the back to show the various tenses of verbs she already knows and uses. Enter two, or at most three, things each time.

Don't try to place pictures in alphabetical order within each letter page; it's far too complicated at this stage.

As she copies the words, make use of the opportunity to stress the initial and final sounds and to let your child hear how you break the word into syllables. This helps with spelling (see pages 133–134). Making a picture dictionary ties in with playing I-Spy types of games (see page 125).

Projects

Projects generally take time and often include several types of activities that, although linked, can be done in different sessions on different days. Projects are often quite complicated, and explanations may have to be given in the child's own language. However, if they are to be a foreign-language learning opportunity, it's necessary to plan beforehand where and what language you are going to use.

As in all activities, projects are most effective if they are well presented, sustained, and followed up. Planning needs time, as it often involves collecting or preparing materials. You may find making a planning sheet, to which you can add ideas as they occur, a helpful aid to thinking a project through.

Cooking

National dishes

Try and make a national dish. It's a good cultural experience and involves new language.

Try something relatively simple such as a Spanish omelet, a German potato salad, or a French onion soup or crêpe. Check the recipe beforehand and write it out step by step for your child to follow. If you need help with cooking language or can't find a recipe, try the library or buy a foreign-language magazine.

If you haven't the time to cook, buy a foreign main dish and dessert at a supermarket. Discuss the names and look for any instructions on the packet in the foreign language. Plan how to prepare the dishes with your child and let her serve them using a little foreign language. Fill in with a few expressions yourself, such as "It's good. Thank you. Pass me . . . " Repeat the meal another time with the same dishes, if they were popular, or try some new ones.

Help your child to make a list of foreign dishes she likes and doesn't like. Make your own list at the same time. Doing this will help prepare her for going to a foreign restaurant with you, either in the U.S. or when you go abroad.

Face biscuits

After you have drawn faces for "I'm happy," "I'm sad," "I'm tired," make some smiling, laughing, and tired face biscuits. Use your usual biscuit recipe and cut out circles to represent the faces. Help your child draw the faces on the biscuits with icing. Add hair to show whether the face is that of a boy or girl. When you eat the biscuits, use the following language: "Can I have him? He's happy. Can I have her? She's sad."

Birthdays

Try and find out how birthdays are celebrated in the foreign country. Learn the "Happy Birthday" song in the foreign language together and help your child make a birthday card using the foreign language. Write labels for the presents in a foreign language and even ice the birthday cake using some foreign language. Play at least one game in the foreign language. Twenty Questions is a good family foreign-language game. The family can ask and you can help your child answer.

Collecting foreign language in your environment

There's probably more foreign language about you than you think. Once you start to look around you, you'll be amazed by what you and your family can collect. Collect all you think will be useful, but target specific language based on themes like clothes, food, and toys.

Places and things to collect

- Labels in international chain stores:
  - —on clothes
  - —on food
  - —on toys
  - —on household goods and furniture
- Newspapers and magazines—different sorts and their price
- Telephone booths—international dialing instructions
- Tourist information about your town or city

Expeditions

Explain to your child the reason for going. Prepare some lists or a questionnaire with interesting things she has to find out. Give her suggestions of what to collect. These might include labels in two languages or a foreign-language magazine. If possible, make sure she gets an opportunity to hear people using the foreign language.

Half-day or day trips can include visits to:

- the airport, including the departure and arrival counters;
- train stations with international connections;
- travel agencies for brochures, foreign railway timetables, etc.;
- exhibitions of foreign products, art, etc.;

- concerts of foreign music;
- films, if suitable;
- the foreign country.

Physical exercises

Build up a little routine of exercises that you do regularly to instructions in the foreign language. Children enjoy it and can take over giving the instructions.

> *"Jump. One, two, three, four. Touch your toes. Down, down, down, now up."*

When your child knows the routine well, make a quite different routine. When she knows both routines well, mix them up without doing the actions yourself. You'll soon find out how much she understands.

Numbers

Playing with numbers is fun in the foreign language if the concepts have already been learned in the child's own language. Start with very simple sums that your child will be sure to get right. In this way the challenge will not be the numbers but matching the foreign language to them.

Oral sums

Begin with oral sums:

> *"2 and 2 make how many?"*
> *"10 minus 3 makes how many?"*

If you don't know the language, buy a foreign-language math book or ask a foreign friend. Go on to playing games such as:

"Think of a number. Add 10. Subtract 6. What's left?"

Written sums

Doing a page of simple sums seems to give children a feeling of satisfaction, but to make it a worthwhile learning experience, write some of the numbers in words not symbols.

Shopping games

Make some shopping games using supermarket advertisements. Give your child 100 francs and ask her how much change she would have if she bought a carton of milk. As she makes more progress, you could give her a written shopping list.

The environment

In preparation for going abroad, you may like to learn some of the foreign-language names for:

- flowers;
- birds;
- trees;
- insects.

After you have talked about them, you could make cards for the memory game or Lotto. Lotto boards could be changed from the usual format to one large picture on each board. For example, a beach scene on one and a mountain scene on another, each with a checklist of six things in a corner of each picture. The scenes would be referred to as "on the beach," "in the mountains," or "in the town." Some of the small cards will have pictures that could apply to each board, for example, a fish; some will have a picture which is only applicable to one—for example, a sandcastle. Instead of placing the cards on the Lotto boards, you can lay them out at the side.

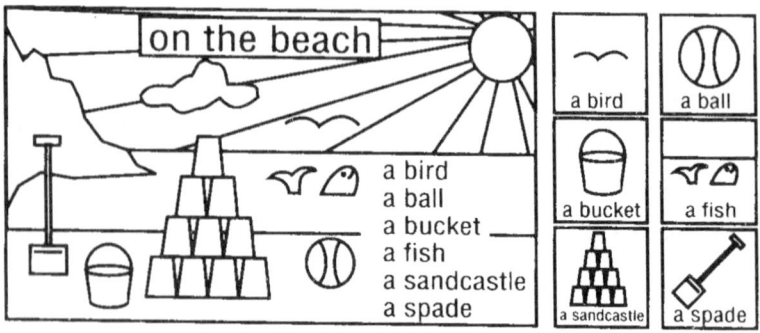

Questions parents ask

> "I'm thinking of arranging a birthday party with a Polish theme for my child. Do you think it's a good idea?"

It could be great but check that your friends feel the same about the foreign language and culture as you and your family. If they don't, the preparations and excitement might bring to the surface some of their prejudices, and it's better not to expose your child to them at this early stage of learning when she's still forming her own attitudes to the culture. Be careful in your choice of country or language for your party or project. You may find that the lack of information about the culture results in over-reliance on stereotypes, some of which you may not feel are appropriate.

Final thoughts

Projects can result in memorable experiences. Like stories, they can be adapted to take on your family flavor and involve the whole family in many different, interesting, and entertaining ways. Successful expeditions increase all-around knowledge as well as providing foreign-learning opportunities. Undertaken together they have lasting effects and remain joint memories long after the children have become adults.

CHAPTER NINE

Selecting materials for you and your child

Both you and your child need materials, but for different reasons. You need materials to create the hands-on experiences through which he learns language. He needs materials because without them he can't get involved in doing things. Materials form the base around which you can build the specific language that your child needs.

Choice of materials

Materials need to be carefully chosen and evaluated. They should:

- help to clarify meaning;
- interest your child enough to maintain his attention;
- provide sufficient challenge to stretch him;
- provide enjoyment and motivation.

The effectiveness of materials depends on the way that you bring them to life for your child. This depends on how you adapt them and personalize them to fit his needs and interests. Many materials are not sufficiently targeted, so time and energy are wasted and progress is therefore slower. Adapting and personalizing is about getting the materials to match your child's level so that he can absorb the language that you are specifically targeting. This is why homemade or home-adjusted materials are often more effective. Don't rely on finding ready-made materials that match your child perfectly. It's very rare that they do. Be prepared to cut and paste and use the photocopier. Once you start doing this, you'll get better and better at it, and you'll be amazed by what you can make your-self and how well it fits your child's needs.

Presentation

Even if the choice of material is right for your child, the material won't be as effective as you hoped if you don't plan how to use it. Materials have to be:

- presented;
- sustained;
- followed up.

You need to plan what language you need for:

- management of the activity;
- specific use with the material.

This does not take long once you get used to it. Much of the planning for the next time is made in evaluating what you've just done together and thinking through the follow-up.

Some parents make the mistake of either:

- presenting too much material in one session so that there isn't time to exploit it to the full;
- only using materials once and so not letting their child get the most from them. Materials can be used successfully a second or even a third time if you present them well. Children like having a second try at most things if you make it fun for them.

There is no hard and fast rule for gauging how much and for how long. It's a skill that you'll develop with experience. You'll find as you get more experienced that you don't need as much material as you first thought. What you will need is plenty of little things for Shorties or the Language Corner to keep up the momentum.

If a child once says, "Oh it's too difficult, I can't understand" and switches off from some material, it is extremely difficult to get him to go back to it. It's best not to try. Just analyze what went wrong. Was it in the choice of materials or in the way you present-ed it? Maybe you hadn't personalized it enough. Although it wasn't a learning experience for your child, make sure it's one for you, and then it's not likely to happen again. Explain to your child that what he was doing was too difficult and take him back to easier, familiar material or new material that you are sure he can do and will enjoy. Like this, you'll gradually build up his confidence.

Types of materials for children

Published

- Books: stories, rhymes, songs, information books, dictionar-ies, dual-language and bilingual books
- Audiocassettes, videocassettes, CD-ROMs, CDs
- Games

Self-made (by you or your child)

- Books
- Puppets
- Games

Real things (realia)

- Concrete objects

Visuals

- Photographs
- Pictures

Human resources

- Other people and children
- Pen pals
- Au pairs

Selecting books

Books can be grouped into the following categories:

- **books with the text translated** but using the same illustrations;
- **books written in the foreign language** with culture-specific illustrations;
- **dual-language books,** where the text is produced in two languages; the illustrations may fit one or both cultures;
- **bilingual books,** where one of the two languages is dominant.

More books written in a foreign language are now available outside their country of origin. However, they are still more easily obtained in the country where they were published. If you or a friend go abroad, make time to stop off in a book store. In a quick visit to the children's section of a book store, you'll find it's possible to collect a selection of books and audiocassettes that will last many sessions of foreign Language Time if properly presented.

Criteria for selection

Apart from interesting your child and offering a further challenge, check the following:

Pictures

- Are they too babyish?
- Can he decode them to understand their meaning?

Children need to be able to decode pictures as well as text. To attract them and hold their interest, both need to communicate some meaningful message that they can understand. Where they can't understand one or both, they switch off, and learning opportunities are lost.

Children find it more difficult than adults imagine to relate to pictures. This is especially the case when their experience has been largely limited to real photography or cartoons, both of which are easier to understand than illustrations. Children need help to decode art nearly as much as they do text. You can do this by careful presentation of pictures, week by week, which you display in the Language Corner. A regular source can be found in newspapers, magazines, and some travel brochures. Don't forget to talk about a picture or pictures in a book. You may have to do this in our own language. If the illustration is by a foreign artist, there y be cultural content that also needs explanation before it can nderstood. You can develop your child's looking skills as well listening skills.

ge

he text spoken-style or written-style language, or both?

ge is too difficult, delay the introduction of the book ference book which can be dipped into for specific oks that have been translated from your own lanful since your child will already know the content understand the foreign language.

llenge,

rge or too small?

Children starting to read a foreign language find it more difficult to decode small print. Small print is also more difficult to copy.

Selecting audiocassettes, videocassettes, CD-ROMs, and CDs

The range available is continually increasing and access is getting easier. The supply can be categorized as follows:

- published for children learning a foreign language;
- published for native-speaker children;
- homemade copies of programs for children learning a foreign language;
- homemade copies of regular programs;
- homemade copies of commercials.

Criteria for selection

Apart from interesting your child and offering a further challenge, check the following:

Language content

- Is there enough language of the kind your child can use?
- Is there too much language?
- Is it bilingual?

Sound effects

- Are there plenty? They help understanding.

Voices

- Are they clear?
- Are the voices natural-sounding and easy to copy?

Film

- Is it fully animated or only partially animated? (Children's expectations are high, as they are influenced by what they see on TV.)

Follow-up material

- What is available? (books, puzzles, games, etc.)

Although recordings are said to be interactive, most don't involve the child in spoken dialogue. It's up to you to turn the passive language your child picks up through listening into active language he can use in dialogue. You can do this by introducing dialogue in linked follow-up activities. If you can't buy any published follow-up materials, make some yourself by cutting up advertising material and finding pictures in magazines, children's newspapers, etc. It takes time to collect material, but if you plan well in advance, you'll have something you can use.

If your child has already read a book or seen a TV program in his own language, let him hear or see it in the foreign language. Help him initially by telling him bits of language he should listen He probably won't get it all the first time so help and encour- him by playing back once (see page 140). If an audio program ts of sound effects, he'll know exactly what part of the story ten to even if he can't understand all the language. It takes uild up to complete understanding, and in some cases it's eave a cassette after several attempts. When you come fter a break, you'll find your child understands much did before. You'll probably be surprised. Don't forget

materials

seful:

ie—dialogues involving telephoning a mes-
fective if you have the right stage props!

- a plastic alphabet—better to buy one made for the foreign language as it will include accents, etc.;
- plastic numbers—it saves time if your child can use ready-made numbers for a game, as having to write them takes time;
- a toy—to be used as a "friend" (see page 58); you might also buy a French doll that says *Papa, Mama, Je m'appelle . . .*, or a German puppet.

Self-made

These can be made by:

- the parent;
- the child;
- both, as a joint venture.

To make something himself rather than using ready-made materials is better for your child, as it involves him at a deeper and more personal level. At the various stages of making the material, there are many different opportunities for him to use language. However, don't let the actual making dominate and detract from using language. It may be better to part-prepare some materials beforehand so that he can get on usefully during Language Time. If you don't do some preparation beforehand cooperate with him during Language Time by sharing the physical tasks like cutting, for example, so that you reach your target more quickly.

Self-made materials can include:

- books;
- games;
- puppets;
- notices;
- lists;
- programs;
- cooking.

Check yourself that your writing or lettering is of a high standard.

Are your handwritten letters the right size and shape? Do you get the right spaces between letters? If not, practice a little before you do some writing for him. It's important to get the right shapes and sizes, as when you begin to read a foreign language you look at detail. Any differences from the standard writing can confuse and make recognizing the letters more difficult. This in turn makes reading text more difficult.

Check that you're making materials the right size for your child to handle and are putting notices at the right height for him to read.

Realia

It takes time to collect realia. Children of seven, eight, and nine enjoy making their own collections, so pass on to your child some of the things you or the family find.

It's not necessary to buy things. A lot of things relating to the foreign language and culture are available in your environment, and they're free. There is probably much more useful material around you than you realize. You've just got to look for it. It's a case of developing a collector's eye! The following suggestions may give you some ideas:

- some catalogs for toys, food, and furniture are now bilingual;
- travel brochures contain photos of food, towns, trains, etc.;
- maps and timetables;
- foreign magazines;
- foreign-language newspapers;
- special promotions of food, etc., for pictures, flags, etc.;
- food products with labels in two or three languages;
- chain supermarkets with trilingual labels on food and clothing.

Ask friends to collect for you when they go abroad. Little things like the following are useful, easily collected, and cost very little or nothing:

- bus and train tickets;
- maps;
- postcards;
- receipts from restaurants;
- menus, place mats, etc., from McDonald's, Pizza Hut, or other international fast-food chains your child knows.

Storing materials

Collect materials as and when you can and store them until you need them. This means working out some place to store materials. Pictures need to be stored flat. If you can classify them as you collect, it will save you a lot of time later. Don't let your child know where you store things, as he'll be sure to find out what you've got, and the novelty will have gone. It's much more fun to keep an element of surprise.

Display

It's important to display things. It motivates your child and involves the family. The standard of your display is important, as it introduces the foreign culture and influences taste. Your choice of pictures will build up an image of the foreign country. How you display them will indicate how you feel about them. A simple mount around a picture or some writing makes both look much more attractive. If it's something your child has done, mount it, too. It'll give him a feeling that you care about it.

It's important to keep changing what you display. You'll probably need some sort of bulletin board in the Language Corner as well as a flat surface. Think of some way to give an overall feel of the country to your Language Corner. Your child can make some flags, or you might pick up some decoration at a food promotion in a local shop.

Materials for parents

You may need materials to help you plan activities and to develop your own language skills.

Planning activities

You may find the following useful:

- a child's foreign-language textbook for your reference;
- rhyme, song, and games books;
- magazines for teachers that include tips for teachers;
- information books that include useful language.

Developing your own language ability and cultural information

Look out for a course on TV or a course with a cassette recording that will help you with spoken language in situations that are useful to you and your child.

Human resources can be very important. Try and find a native speaker who would help with spoken child's language and also be willing to record audiocassettes for you.

Questions parents ask

<u>"I have no time to collect realia as I work all day."</u>

Here are a few suggestions that might help you:

- Visit the newsstand and get a magazine, preferably a foreign one, and start cutting and pasting. Send for travel brochures.
- You can make some games with glue, scissors, and colored pencils. The insides of cereal boxes, show boxes, etc., are a source of cardboard.

- Recruit the help of other members of your family. Tell them the kind of thing you need.
- Ask your child to look for books about the country when he goes to the library.
- Telephone a bookstore and ask if they have any foreign language rhyme and storybooks. They may have a catalog they can send you.

Final thoughts

Your choice of materials and the variety to which you expose your child will contribute to his all-around development. Not only will he learn how to learn from things other than written text, he will find out about another culture. The selection and quality of materials to which you expose him will develop his artistic sense. They will also help to form his impression of the foreign country, its people, and their language and culture.

CHAPTER TEN

Planning language opportunities outside the home and abroad

If you have started off your child in a foreign language at home, there comes a time when you feel she needs to broaden her experience beyond what you can offer. You may feel the same about the lessons at school or the foreign-language club. Some kind of total-immersion experience, beyond the guided total-immersion experiences you have organized, can take her on to a higher learning plateau. It may also remotivate what may be by now a slightly flagging interest.

On the face of it, a foreign-language experience sounds like a wonderful idea. How many parents have already imagined the progress their child will make before she's even left the house? But be cautious—things can go wrong. The whole experience can sometimes be quite disastrous, and if that's the case, it takes time and patience to put things back on the right track.

Before you decide to let your child go on a foreign experience, check carefully into all the details and weigh the disadvantages as well as the advantages for her. If you have doubts that it is right for your child, and your family's principles, have the courage to look for or plan something else. It will be worth it in the long run.

Among the things worth considering are:

- What will my child get out of it? How much will she use the foreign language? Will she be able to make friends and belong to a group?
- Will it be compatible with our family's ethos and attitudes?
- What quality of intercultural exchange will there be?

Types of foreign-language experiences

- Exchange between two families
- Family holiday
- School journey for skiing or tourism, or a school exchange

Whatever the type of trip, even if it is arranged by the school, it is worthwhile doing your own preparation at home. The potential of any overseas language experience can't be even partially achieved without careful preparation and follow-up. A child who is well prepared starts off with confidence and is better equipped to cope with the cultural differences and surprises.

Presentation

The way you present the idea of going abroad is important. Some children are excited by the novelty; others don't want to go. They're comfortable at home and can't stand the idea of missing their favorite TV programs.

It's important that your child understands:

- the reason for going;
- what you hope she will achieve;
- her new responsibilities—money from other countries, telephone card, etc.;

- her precise tasks—for example, things to get for the family: stamps for brother, a doll for baby sister, etc.
- things to find out for the family—new recipes, for example.

If you personalize the experience when you present it, your child will immediately become involved. She'll feel that she's been made responsible for doing something for herself as well as the family. This will probably make her feel quite mature, as what she sees as an adult role of bringing back information and things for the family has been delegated to her.

Planning

Many a good learning opportunity abroad has been wasted because there wasn't sufficient planning beforehand. Leading up to an experience can be just as important as the actual experience.

Planning depends on finding out information beforehand and collecting as many materials as you can about the journey, the place, the people, the food, and so on. If your child is staying with a family, it's essential to find out about the family. Remember that where there are younger children in a family, your child is likely to use more language. Younger children ask a lot of things, and they'll expect her to reply. Through the materials you collect, prepare your child, step by step, on what to expect and how to cope. You'll lessen the culture shock and provide her with a familiar base from which she can begin to explore her new environment. Don't do everything yourself. Many things you can do together such as booking tickets and checking travel times and working out costs by converting prices.

Planning should also include information on daily life, such as what to expect each day and at about what time. Meal times can be very different, and some children find getting used to new times difficult. They get hungry. Getting-up times and bathroom routines may be different, too. Try and find out all you can. Where you don't know, tell your child to copy the other children in the family if it seems reasonable. Tell her that if she's completely lost just to sit down and read a book until someone tells her what's next on the program.

She'll also need the necessary survival language to go with daily life. Has she ever asked you in a foreign language, "Can I go to the bathroom, please?" or had to tell you, "I feel sick"? Does she know how they'll ask her if she wants some more dessert and what she says in reply? Tell her how to say "It was very good."

Teach her little politenesses such as how to address people in the foreign language. In Europe and South America these may include shaking hands first thing in the morning and when a visitor comes to the house. The good-night routine may also be more formal. Prepare her for the frequent custom of kissing good night on either or both cheeks. In Japan she'll be expected to take her shoes off in the little hall before she goes into the house and put on house slippers. She'll also be expected to change her house slippers to bathroom slippers before she goes into the toilet. Before she actually begins to use her chopsticks she'll be expected to say "Itadakimasu"—"Thank you for what I'm going to have." If she's prepared for these more formalized rituals, she'll find it easier to fit in and copy how the other children do things.

If you are going on a family vacation, it's nice for your child to play with other children on the beach or in the swimming pool. Don't expect her to organize this herself. It usually doesn't happen that way, as most children are shy about approaching other children they don't know, and even more so if they speak another language. Go with her and talk to the other children. Explain where you come from and tell them your child's name. Take a football or some other game with you and ask them if they would like to play or, if it seems right, ask them if she could join in their game. It probably won't go so well the first time, but try and meet them again. Your child will find that things will go better the next time and she can manage by herself and the other children may even start to call her by her name. Listen to their language and, at some other time, go over it with your child so she'll be able to understand most of what they're saying.

Sustaining interest—on an exchange

If your child is on an exchange, she might not want you to get in contact with her. This is quite usual if things are going well. In her new world, life is busy with new experiences, and while the novelty lasts, she may be embarrassed if you contact her. It's up to you though—you know your child and whether she needs you to make contact first. If and when she contacts you, don't scold her for her silence. You've probably been missing her more than she has you, as her new life is busy and different. When she contacts you, it's vital to be positive and encouraging. Don't dwell on the differences and difficulties, which she may recount in detail. Try and take her beyond them to thinking about the tasks you've asked her to do for you and the family.

Sustaining interest—on vacation

Even if you're on a family vacation, your child's interests need to be encouraged and sustained. Recap what you've achieved together and listen attentively to her impressions and feelings. It's important to her, and she may have a different and interesting way of looking at things. Praise her on how much language she's used so far and help her with new phrases, suggesting when she can use them. Ask her to tell you any new language she's picked up. There may be some new words and expressions you don't know—or you can pretend you don't know—to make her feel good. Discuss ideas for new expeditions and let her help you in making the plans, buying the tickets, and even interpreting directions and explanations. Although it's easier and faster to do everything yourself, don't— you're depriving your child of a chance to learn.

> *After six days in Paris, an American boy, aged nine, was asked by an American lady sitting at the next table, "Do you know any French?"*
>
> *The mother quickly replied, "No, he doesn't. We don't speak French." The lady continued talking to the boy, "Do you know any French words?"*
>
> *"No, he can't speak French," his mother replied, before her son had time to reflect and reply.*
>
> *"Do you know how to say yes and no in French?" the lady persisted.*
>
> *"Yes, he does," his mother replied, "But he's very tired. We've been here six days."*
>
> *A soda was then served to the boy, and he said nothing, not even* merci *(thank you, in French).*

Each day, plan more language and help your children to use it.

Revisit places or shops; children often enjoy going back to something they know. But have some specific aim for a second visit—for example, to buy something, collect some historical details, or take some extra photographs.

Play games such as I-Spy or the first to see ten car license plates beginning with 6. Of course, you have to say the numbers in the foreign language!

Plan a special expedition:

- to a nearby town to spend extra pocket money;
- a journey by ship;
- play a new sport.

Telephone the grandparents.

Buy interesting postcards and send them to family and friends.

Try and find some new challenges. Plan an expedition day when you go further afield. If you make it sound interesting and fun, you'll enjoy it and learn some new things. Plan I-Spy type games and take a cassette for a sing-along during the car journey.

You could make a day's journey to cross a frontier—for example, from Calais, France, to Bruges, Belgium. This could involve a surprising amount of new language as well as cultural contrasts.

- You can study maps to find the exact position of the boundary—by a small stream, a river, or a ditch, perhaps;
- You can make checklists of visual symbols indicating the change of country; these could include frontier posts, road signs, language, money, stores, gas stations, car number plates, uniforms, and styles of dress.

In your enthusiasm, don't forget that you should all be having a good time. Engineer experiences so that they look as if they happened quite naturally. Spend more time talking to local people than you might at home. Ask the way to shops, ask the ticket collector what time he opens in the morning and if he's open tomorrow. Although you can see the list of ice creams, ask the sales person what flavors he's got. By doing this, your child will have a chance to hear more language.

If things go wrong, try not to complain too much. Your child will already be disappointed, and if you dwell on the topic too long, it can influence her attitudes. Children are impressionable and may not realize that your feelings are only temporary.

A checklist for a family vacation to a hotel or rented accommodation (check the boxes)

Preparation

Journey
- [ ] length of time, length in miles and kilometers
- [ ] route—Make a list of the main towns, which can be checked and crossed off on the way.

Map
- [ ] Mark out the journey.
- [ ] Check any differences in writing names (for example, *Vienna/Wien*, *Liège/Luik*).
- [ ] Note the frontiers.

Money
- [ ] Check currency lists at the bank (currency name and flag).
- [ ] Obtain some currency—check names, values of notes and coins, equivalence in dollars.

Telephone
- [ ] country codes, town codes, local numbers
- [ ] international codes, emergency phone numbers

Food
- [ ] typical dishes, cooking a dish, or trying a restaurant
- [ ] comparing international food-chain menus

Weather
- [ ] Check latitudes and compare them (for example, Cannes and Prague).
- [ ] Check temperatures—compare towns.
- [ ] Check international weather charts in the newspaper.

On site

Shopping
- ☐ toys and puzzles
- ☐ books, magazines, and comics
- ☐ videos (borrow videos for early morning listening)
- ☐ souvenirs

Tourism
- ☐ historical sites
- ☐ markets
- ☐ nature parks

Food
- ☐ snacks
- ☐ ice cream
- ☐ cafés and restaurants

Sports
- ☐ water and beach sports, skiing, etc.

Prepare your child to collect materials by making large envelopes into which things can be easily slotted.
- ☐ tickets
- ☐ supermarket and store receipts
- ☐ menus and place mats if you can collect them
- ☐ postcards with recipes

See that your child has the right kind of survival language to use:
- ☐ on the journey
- ☐ in daily life
- ☐ shopping
- ☐ playing games and sports

Follow-up

The excitement of a vacation lasts for a relatively short time on your return. Try and catch the mood and use it for follow-up. Make a picture vacation album using photos, postcards, maps, and any other worthwhile realia. Write a few thank-you postcards, if it's appropriate. They could be a way of cementing a friendship. Although follow-up activities provide good opportunities to practice new language, don't push too hard or you'll kill some of the vacation fun.

Things to make and do

- Make a souvenir book or albums for you or the family to put in the Language Corner.
- Talk about where to go next time and what to do.
- Write labels (To _____ From _____) on souvenirs in the foreign language.
- Write thank-you letters.
- Send postcards to friends.
- Cook a favorite dish or cake.
- Read new storybooks and listen to audiocassettes.
- Watch new videos.

If the stay abroad has been a worthwhile experience, your child is probably ready to move on to language experiences beyond the home. Start checking the range of availability, using the same criteria for selection as you did for your child's stay abroad (see page 163).

Pen-pal clubs

It is possible to start off a pen-pal exchange on an individual basis or as a group. The individual basis might result from a holiday friendship or someone you have contacted through a pen-pal society (see page 207).

It's fun to make a pen-pal exchange in a group. Pen-pal groups have been organized through churches, out-of-school clubs, and through sister-city associations.

Once you've started a pen-pal relationship, it's quite difficult to keep it going. Letters should include plenty of pictures so that writing doesn't become too burdensome. Write in a spoken style rather than written, as this is much easier for children. Some children write letters that are comiclike in appearance, with the language in spoken style in speech bubbles. It's best to have some sort of plan for exchanging information. Suggest one or two topics each time. If you've got some special news, abandon the plan for a session, but go back to it for the next letter.

Topics for pen-pal letters

Yourself

- things you can and can't do (riding a bicycle, skating, playing the violin)
- things and people you like and don't like
- Ask them to tell you about themselves.

Your family and pets

- people
- occupations
- birthdays

Your school

- lessons you enjoy
- sports you enjoy
- friends
- teachers
- expeditions

Your town

- Make maps.
- Show pictures of important places, transport, etc.

Simulated overseas experiences

It may be that your child needs to broaden her experience, but it is not possible for you to send her abroad, or she may not be ready to go by herself. If this is the situation, try and find a total-immersion experience run by a native speaker in your neighborhood. If nothing exists try and start something yourself with the help of a parent or native speaker.

Simulated overseas experiences may be better for some children, as they don't involve the insecurity of leaving home. They may also serve as a useful bridge to going abroad at a later stage.

Ballet, swimming, or sports in a foreign language

Language is easier when it's linked to physical movement. You may find a native speaker who is already running classes in English. Try and persuade her to start a small group in the foreign language. If you go skiing, you could try to find a ski school in the foreign language for your child—she'll soon pick up the language to go with skiing and probably make some foreign friends, too.

A foreign-language swap shop or mini-library

Foreign-language materials are difficult to find—and are expensive. People who have finished with materials may be pleased to exchange them for something different. Together with a native-speaker friend, organize a private foreign-language swap shop once or twice a month. Make it a total-immersion foreign-language experience. Don't let the adults organize the swaps among themselves. Get them to work together with their children. Like this, adults and children will all get a chance to use the foreign language.

Swaps can include:

- picture books, information books, rhyme and song books;
- audiocassettes;
- magazines;
- comics.

This can develop into a mini-library, if there is a base of materials. The native speaker may, as she gets to know the children, begin to talk to them about the books. This type of presentation helps them to select and encourages them to go beyond their usual reading interests. You might encourage her to tell a story—which you should record on cassette—and play some games. You might even go as far as to celebrate birthdays.

Final thoughts

Where foreign travel is successful, it broadens and motivates. After a stay abroad, children's outlook and attitudes are changed. However, care has to be taken that foreign travel doesn't serve as an opportunity to confirm prejudices and self-fulfilling prophecies that have been acquired from peers and other adults and may lie hidden beneath the surface. Simulated, overseas total-immersion experiences can be substituted for foreign travel and may well be more suitable for some children at certain stages of development and in special circumstances.

CHAPTER ELEVEN

Culture awareness and culture shock

What is culture? Why is it important?

When we say we understand what a foreign-language speaker says to us, how much do we really understand? You might think you understand words such as *bread* or *bath*, but is the image in the other person's mind the same as yours?

> *"She understands the words, but not the implications behind them,"*
> *her mother said, talking about her fifteen-year-old Chinese daugh-*
> *ter, who was learning English in an American junior high school.*

Culture has been constructed by people and has to be learned. You can't communicate effectively, even about concrete everyday things, without making some attempt to understand the culture behind the words. Interaction depends on the attributed meaning of the word coinciding with the intended meaning. Where the two don't coincide, misunderstandings can arise. How many people have suffered from believing that the equivalent to *Yes* in Japanese is *Hai*, only to find out that there had been no agreement, only an acknowledgment that the listener had heard what was said?

Language and culture are interrelated. The young child learns culture and language simultaneously while doing things. No materials are culture-free. If he is exposed to cultural experiences, he absorbs culture without realizing it. Through talking with people, he encounters their view of the world, which they express through the language they use. Where he's exposed to two cultures—for example, when he's living abroad—he recognizes what belongs to the foreign culture and soon learns how to adapt to that culture.

A young child is generally a shrewd observer and soon picks up the body language belonging to the foreign language, if he's exposed to native speakers.

> *An American girl, aged seven, returning to America having attended Japanese school in Tokyo, found it difficult to speak to the teacher and look her in the eyes when she spoke. She wasn't used to the informality. In Japan, when she did speak to her teacher, she would keep her head down and use polite forms of language, adding* teacher *in Japanese to what she said.*

After some time in total immersion, a young child is capable of comparing and contrasting certain things in the two cultures. His degree of observation is often quite surprising and sometimes amusing, too. But for the young child it's serious. He hardly ever makes any judgment about other cultures. He doesn't think of them in terms of being right or wrong, good or bad unless adults have put these ideas into his head. He's curious and interested. Perhaps one of the greatest contributions parents can make is to keep alive this open prejudice-free interest in other cultures.

You may think that finding out more about the culture is not worth the effort as, by the time your child is grown up, the international or global culture will be more important. Transnational companies are flooding the world markets with their products, but to what extent does global sameness exist in what they market? Many a child's face changes when he takes his first bite of his favorite burger abroad. The visual image of the fast-food restaurant is reassuringly the same worldwide, but the taste isn't. Cultural tastes dictate, and for success the global burger, although the same in size, shape, and even sometimes name, has been adapted to accommodate the local palate.

At first glance eight- and nine-year-olds in Paris and London playing football in a park look the same. They're dressed in the same uniforms and sports gear. However, on closer inspection you'll notice the difference in hair styles and the use of body language. And what about how they play? The relationships between the players don't seem quite the same. And what about the concept of fair play? The English words *le fair play* are used in French, but can the activity transfer without some local cultural input?

> *The Asian lady loved the homemade chocolate cake so much that when asked if she would like a second piece she accepted with pleasure. Having finished it, she asked if she might have another piece: a third helping. Imagine the surprise of everyone having tea. Finally she asked if she could have the last piece. After finishing her fourth helping she added, "You see, I finished it to show you how delicious I thought it was." The reaction of the English adults and children was quite different. They had all been brought up to feel that a second helping was the limit. Beyond that it was greed—one of the biblical seven sins. In their minds their Asian guest was greedy, and that was bad. Alas, the attributed meaning didn't coincide with the Asian guest's intended meaning.*

Culture is all about how groups of people understand and interpret the world and solve problems. It is multilayered, but only the outer layers are explicit. These consist of things that can be seen, such as historical monuments, buildings, churches and shrines, art, food, and transport systems. Most of us have visual images of these kinds of things stored in our minds as representing the culture of that country. In fact, these images are symbols of a deeper invisible culture.

The middle layers consist of norms and values. Norms represent the group's principles of right and wrong, which are controlled by laws and social conventions. Values are the group's concepts of good and bad. They reveal the group's aspirations and hopes. In many cultures the middle layers are influenced and even tied to systems of education and religion. This may still be so where the overt practices of religion apparently have been abandoned, as religion is still part of history.

The inner core is implicit. It's about how the group survives the elements of nature and its effect on the environment. It is concerned with coping strategies in earthquake zones, tropical or Mediterranean climates, severe winters with little daylight, the four seasons in Northern Europe, and so on. It consists of the basic assumptions about life; the unquestioned routine solutions to daily life problems that are accepted, taken for granted, and not discussed. It is essential to refer back to this inner core of human existence if we want to begin to understand the basic differences between cultures.

Culture forms the roots of all our actions, although we are generally not aware of its role. It's often not until we come in contact with a different culture that we begin to examine our own and think beyond the visible layers.

If children are to grow up into sensitive, open-minded adolescents and adults who are sympathetic to other cultures and willing to find out more, it is important to lay foundations in the attitude-forming years of childhood.

Planning

It is important to be positive about all you do and say as you are influencing lifelong attitudes.

*Amy, the girl next door, moved to Tokyo with her parents
and wrote regularly to her next-door friend, Marge, aged
eight, sending her little gifts, stamps, and even a kimono and
geta (Japanese shoes). This left Marge with lifelong, positive
attitudes to all things Japanese. When Marge went to college,
she took a Japanese language course. While on vacation, she
traveled to Japan but found it different from the stereotypes
she had built up in her mind. Her positive attitudes and
studies helped her over this disappointment. Today, she
works in the field of Japanese studies.*

Plan to guide your child beyond the outer layers of the culture and
help him to begin to find out about the inner layers. It may be too
early to discuss comparisons, but he'll be storing information for
later when, with more experience and greater maturity, he'll begin
to understand the reasons for specific cultural behavior.

Start by looking at the foreign-language culture. Don't be
tempted to launch into multiculturalism, as it makes learning more
difficult. It can come later. Through comparison and contrast of
the foreign culture with his own, he will build up his own systems
for analyzing culture. At the same time he'll be finding out about
his own culture: something he probably was unaware of before. He
needs time to develop his own systems of analysis before he is
ready to tackle a third culture in depth. Of course, he can do it, but
it will probably slow down his learning and might also confuse.
Through activities aim to:

- encourage curiosity;
- develop empathy for other peoples;
- respect other ways of doing things;
- look for similarities as well as differences;
- understand that the value of words may differ between
  cultures;
- develop awareness of his own culture.

A young child's developing understanding of the value of words

A British girl, aged five, who was learning French, passed through these stages:

Stage 1

The child admitted that the two words could be used to describe the same thing.

a car

une voiture

Step 2

Three months later she worked out for herself that the relationship of concrete things is not always one to one. There is some cultural input that can alter things. She had never seen a notebook that looked like a French *cahier*.

a notebook	*plain or lined paper*
un cahier	*different size, with squared paper and a ruled margin*

Step 3

school lunch	*meat, two vegetables, and cookies, served by cafeteria staff*
repas de midi	*a three-course meal with sauces and dessert*

She gradually began to work out that the attributed meaning of words was not always their real or intended meaning.

How to help

Presentation and discussion are important if your child's positive attitudes are to be encouraged and developed. These have to take place in your child's own language and are best done at other times than Language Times, when you're trying to create a total-immersion experience. Materials provide a base around which you can build discussion. They may be visual but can take children beyond the outer layers of culture. Weather charts, maps for checking the position on the globe, temperature scales, and current news about earthquakes, for example, can be starting points for looking at the influences on the inner core of culture.

Since language and culture are interrelated in activities, the child will pick up both. It is up to you, therefore, to plan some activities that include more culture than others, such as making Chinese fried rice and eating it with chopsticks, or singing a German action song. The following lists may help to start you thinking about targeting cultural content. Although they are listed as outer and inner layers of culture, in reality the division is in the adult mind, as the two are intertwined and overlap. Many other ideas are mentioned throughout the book, especially in chapters 9 and 10.

Outer-layer culture

What does it look like?

- Use visuals—photographs of towns, the countryside, people, and types of housing and gardens.
- Use stories and talk about places and people of historical interest.

What does it sound like?

- Use recordings of music, songs, dance (folk), and rhymes.

What does it taste like?

- Investigate food and cooking.

Inner-layer culture

What does it feel like?

- Use weather maps.
- Look for the country on the globe.

Way of life

- Daily life
- Family life
- School life
- Leisure time activities

Stereotypes

Whether it's good to use stereotypes or not is open to debate. However, within reason, and if used sensitively, they have their place and value, providing they are reasonably up-to-date and not an overexaggeration.

All English men don't wear bowler hats. They never did, and to see a bowler being worn in the City of London today is rare. All French men don't wear berets. All German men don't wear leather trousers. All Spaniards don't wear sombreros. Some Japanese children have never put on a kimono.

It is important not to introduce your child to out-of-date extremes that record what surprises rather than what is familiar. Although these types of stereotypes persist, they're best avoided. If you can't avoid them, take time to explain them and so diminish their importance.

Stereotypes are broad generalizations. They are useful in that they provide an essential simplified form or symbol that can be immediately understood and learned. Stereotypes are like stepping stones. They provide a way into the culture. With greater experience they may be found not to be truly representative of the culture and consequently may be discarded.

Child culture

Child culture exists in every society. The place given to the child within the family and society differs from culture to culture, as do the expectations of what the child can or should do. It's difficult to find out about child culture—the typical games, the daily life at home and at school, and the relationship between parents, extended family, and the child.

Try to find out through books, asking people, or watching if you go abroad. The more playground games and child language your child knows, the easier it will be for him to play with other children when he goes abroad. He'll have some common ground. The more you can prepare him for daily life and especially table culture—food and manners—the more you'll all enjoy your holiday abroad. In many European countries, for example, children are welcomed into restaurants, even at night, but it is accepted that they know how to manage in such situations.

School life

School life can be very different from country to country. It's useful to find out as much as you can about it as it influences children's way of thinking as well as behavior. Not only may the content and way of instruction differ, but so can expectations. How do children talk to their teacher, and how do teachers expect children to reply? Teacher-child relations differ from culture to culture and this can cause problems even in a classroom in your own country where the native-speaker teacher expects children to behave as in her own country—and they don't.

Body language

This differs from culture to culture. Talk to your child about it so that he's not too surprised or embarrassed by different forms of physical contact such as shaking hands, kissing on both cheeks, and direct eye contact. Touching and physical closeness—or the opposite—can upset children if they're not prepared for it.

Culture shock

Culture shock in adults is accepted, but few people realize that children can also suffer from it. They think that children take a change of country and way of life in their stride. This may be because young children cannot express in words how they feel, and many don't even understand what's upsetting them. To adults everything looks fine because their children are busily occupied.

Culture shock is not only experienced in a change of country. A degree of culture shock may be felt when a child moves to a new area or goes to a new place on vacation within your own country. In these cases the shock is probably less and certainly more easily absorbed, as there is no language barrier, and cultural similarities are soon discovered.

Culture shock in moving to a foreign country seems to pass from a honeymoon stage, when the foreign culture is a novelty, to a stage of frustration, when cultural differences loom larger than similarities. Periods of frustration can be minimized if a child is equipped with knowledge about the culture and way of life, as this information helps to provide him with clues to decoding the culture. Visual images of the new culture seem to contribute to lessening culture shock for children. Matching familiar scenes of the new culture with the reality on arrival make acceptance of change more rapid. The time the child has before his move to ponder over the visuals, show them to his family and friends, and talk about them, helps him to allay fears, and this contributes to his ability to adapt quickly.

Japanese children who have been sent photos of their new house, school, and teachers in the U.S. settle in more rapidly than those for whom everything on arrival is completely new. They can recognize their new home from the outside and already know what their own room looks like.

What children expect depends on the culture they come from. Prior knowledge helps them to identify the reassuring similarities on which they can construct their understanding of the foreign culture. Once over the frustration, children move on to the third stage of enjoyment and acceptance. You can help to minimize culture shock for your child by helping him to build up his personal bank of cultural information. In this way he will be prepared for eventual encounters with the culture, such as visiting a foreign restaurant, meeting people from other countries, or coping when he goes abroad.

Questions parents ask

"How can I find out more about Spanish culture— especially the inner layers?"

Ask at the library for books on Spain and especially on the Spanish and Spanish society. Watch out for programs on television and radio or cultural programs and lectures in your own. If you can find a Spanish family living locally, this will give you a firsthand opportunity to find out about their way of life and what they think about their host country's culture. Their comments will probably be thought-provoking.

"My child comes back from school with ideas about another culture that I don't like."

Among children cultural prejudices spread rapidly, and what peers say is influential. Prejudices are usually based on the visual symbolic layers of culture. Try and explain why these symbols are as they are. Your child will begin to understand the reality, and although he may be too shy to contradict his peers, he'll probably discard their point of view.

Final thoughts

Interest and curiosity about the foreign culture can serve to motivate language learning. In discovering more about another culture, your child will learn how to identify aspects of his own culture and understand it better. The systems for analyzing culture, which children work out for themselves, are fundamental in understanding the implications behind actions and language. Many bilingual and bicultural children are known to grow up to be skilled at international negotiating. They are said to "understand the way of thinking behind the words."

CHAPTER TWELVE

Keeping the foreign language alive

Languages are for life. Language skills learned in childhood don't ever seem to be completely forgotten, they just get rusty. It's like riding a bicycle or swimming, once you can do it, you never forget completely, and with practice it comes back.

Keeping a foreign language alive appears to be linked to the ability to read. Children who have not started to read in the foreign language lose their spoken ability very quickly if they're not given opportunities to use it. Children who have become quite good speakers and can read manage to keep some of their language ability. The degree to which they keep it, however, depends on the level of their spoken and reading ability. Of course, whatever their reading level, children lose some of their ability if they don't have opportunities to hear, speak, and read the language. If they continue just reading, they keep something, but they lose confidence in their ability to speak; consequently, when confronted with an opportunity to speak, they end up by saying nothing, very little or just giggling.

A British girl aged 11, fluent in her second language, French, had difficulty in learning German declensions and grammar from the text book at secondary school. Finally she asked her parents to find her a German family with whom she could

> *stay. She promised she would come back speaking German, as she said this was the way she learned. After a two-week stay, there was a marked change in her spoken ability and attitude. She had proved to herself that she knew how to learn languages and it wasn't the way she was being taught at school.*

If your child is not yet reading or just beginning to read the foreign language, and if you don't want her to lose this ability, it's essential to keep up some activities. If you can't manage to do so yourself, and you can't find anything near home, she'll lose her ability fairly rapidly. Of course she'll retain the positive attitudes you've developed together. Later, when she restarts learning, she'll learn surprisingly quickly and more quickly than children learning a foreign language for the first time. This will certainly be the case if, when she restarts, you support and encourage her at home.

If your child is already reading, it's a pity not to let her continue some activities. After a great effort prior to a vacation or a winter of Language Times, it's understandable that you may feel you would like a break. If this is the case, look around for a good French Club or a total-immersion experience (see page 51), but continue informal Shorties and stories and keep the Language Corner. If she asks to do things in the foreign language, make time and encourage her. During school holidays, try to do one or two projects. You'll all enjoy them and they'll probably help to keep the family involved. Since you've gotten into the habit of planning and collecting materials, it's quite easy to keep something going and, even if it involves going over old ground, your child won't mind.

You have already invested a lot of time in your child, and it's worth persisting further. Continue showing interest in what she's doing and continue sharing some things together. If you hand over everything to other adults outside the family, your child may get the impression that you and the family don't care any more about the foreign language. This could be damaging and affect later foreign-language learning. It could also influence her attitudes to the foreign culture.

Which foreign language at secondary school?

There may be a choice of what language to learn at primary or secondary school. Before you make a decision, it's important to talk it over with your child, bearing in mind the following:

- All foreign-language classes will start right from the beginning. They will teach spoken language and include a grammatical analysis. The language taught, as well as the grammar terminology, may be different from what she's learned and may confuse her. This could result in loss of confidence and could eventually demotivate, but it depends on your child and how you approached the language.
- Most teachers find it difficult to cater to the needs of individual children who have already learned the foreign language and are at different levels of fluency. This often results in their becoming bored and demotivated.
- What other languages do they teach? How do they teach them? Are there opportunities to meet foreign nationals or visit the country?
- Would it be better to start a third language?

Third-language learning

It is now accepted that learning a third language is much easier than learning a second, provided the learning methods and opportunities are similar.

A Canadian girl, aged fourteen, fluent in French and English and attending a French government school abroad, started to learn German at school. The woman teacher taught it like Latin, making the children learn declensions and grammar from the textbook. The girl was used to picking up languages and found she couldn't learn German this way. Her mother understood and arranged for her to stay, during the holidays, with a German family who had two young children. She rapidly picked up spoken German and proved to herself that she could learn German easily but not the way she was being taught at school.

Children learn their third language in much the same way they learned their first and second. Their language-learning habits have been tried and developed. They approach learning a third language with confidence and interest. Their experience with two languages has given them an insight into how language works. This gives them a head start over other children learning their first foreign language. They generally manage to achieve good accents too, as they have two repertoires of sounds on which to drawn.

If the third language comes from the same linguistic base (for example French, Spanish, and Italian all share Latin origins), it is easier to learn. However, where the language has different origins —the structure and, in some languages, the writing form both being different—children still take learning a third language in their stride. In fact, they seem to enjoy the challenge of a third language with a different script.

Adults learning to write Arabic as a third language found the change in flow from right to left involved the use of new muscles and eye-hand coordination that was sometimes painful. Children aged eight to ten for whom Arabic was their first foreign language had no apparent difficulties. In the same group, following the same course, the children learned faster than their parents.

Selecting a third language

If your child has a good base in her first language, it may be better for you to discuss with her the idea of starting a third language— her second foreign language—when she enters secondary school. She would be starting from the beginning with the other children and would therefore be at the same level as the others in the class. It is thought that it is easier to start the difficult foreign languages early, so this may be the right time to start a language such as Russian, Chinese, Japanese, or Arabic. Find out from the school how it teaches the language, what its program is, and if the language can be taken for examinations. All this is important as, once started, your child needs to be able to continue the language and, if it's a difficult language, you are not very likely to be able to do this at home.

If she isn't interested in a difficult language, or there is no opportunity to learn one at the school, you could suggest that if she has been learning a Latin-based language at home, she should start German, or vice versa. This is likely to lead to less confusion as the languages are so different. If she has learned a Latin-based language with you, she can pick up another Latin-based language in the future with relative ease, providing she is motivated to study. If other world languages are taught at school, you might consider starting one of these, but discuss it together first.

Learning a third language and keeping the second

If your child starts to learn her third foreign language at school (where it is classed as a second language), it is up to you to search for ways for her to continue her second foreign language. You can't expect her to do it herself. If you don't find some interesting ways of keeping it, after some initial enthusiasm, it will be pushed to one side.

- Ask if there's a foreign-language club she can join at school. This could be fun. They might welcome her knowledge, and she could meet others, who like her, have also learned at home. This could lead to all kinds of motivating activities.
- Check if there are any total-immersion programs locally. Contact the relevant embassy's cultural institute and see what programs it runs during the school year and holidays.

There may be more going on locally, or a short journey away, than you realize.

- At the same time, try to keep some things going in the family. As she is now older, she most likely won't want to settle down to Language Times, but she'll probably like you to spare time to talk with her about what she is doing.
- She'll probably enjoy opportunities to listen to music, so you could try and introduce her to foreign-language pop. It is possible to buy CDs or cassettes here, even if you can't stock up with them abroad.
- Go to a foreign restaurant from time to time together and try to persuade her to help you make some foreign dishes for the family.
- She may still have her pen pal, which provides another chance to use the language.
- Record foreign-language films on video or borrow foreign-language videos for her and get her magazines or a book she can read. Try to look at them together and talk over things that will interest her.
- If you're planning a vacation, even if it's just a couple of nights away, select a destination where she can use her second language. Make sure she's involved in the planning and does some of the interpreting for you. If she's ready for it, plan an exchange (page 166).

Leave any messages, including telephone messages, for her in the foreign language, pinned to the Language Corner board.

If you search, there are many opportunities through which you and the family can help her keep alive the language she knows. However, all these opportunities will be more beneficial to your child if you discuss them with her. In this way you repeat and extend the opportunities to use the foreign language and continue to influence her understanding and attitudes toward the culture.

Final thoughts

Languages are for life, and they can't be taken away from you once you've learned them. By helping your child and continuing to help her, you'll have made a lasting contribution to her quality of life and understanding of others and their culture.

From your beginnings at home, she is ready and confident to go on to study a third or even later a fourth language. For her, languages are real and living. They're a means of communicating with other people.

Through learning about another culture, she has learned to look at her own. This provides her with the tools for looking at yet other cultures and so helps her develop a multicultural outlook.

Through your careful planning and sharing of time, you've broadened your child's outlook, increased her knowledge, and through working together you have developed her skills in learning how to learn.

By starting young, she's taken all this in her stride. Although at times, especially during adolescence, she may appear to devalue her foreign-language skills, with maturity she'll discover the possibilities these offer her on the road ahead. It's perhaps only then that you'll fully realize the contribution you have made.

Useful phrases for beginning French, German, Spanish, and Italian

French

About me

My name is . . .	Je m'appelle . . .
I'm . . .	Je suis . . .
I'm eight.	J'ai huit ans.
My birthday is on October 1st.	Mon anniversaire est le 1er octobre.
I like playing football.	J'aime jouer au football.
I like watching television.	J'aime regarder la télevision (or) la télé.
I don't like swimming.	Je n'aime pas nager.
Do you like cooking?	Aimes-tu faire la cuisine?
It's great.	C'est super.
I don't like it.	Je n'aime pas ça.
I've got a watch.	J'ai une montre.

I'm wearing my red socks today.	Je porte mes chausettes rouges aujourd'hui.
My T-shirt is dirty.	Mon T-shirt est sale.
Have you got a bag?	As-tu un sac?
That's my book.	C'est mon livre.
Is that yours?	C'est à toi?
I don't like chocolate.	Je n'aime pas le chocolat.
Do you like ice cream?	Aimes-tu la glace?
What's the matter?	Qu'est ce qu'il y a?
I feel sick.	Je ne me sens pas bien. Je me sens malade.
I've got a headache.	J'ai mal à la tête.
I'm tired.	Je suis fatigué(e).
I'm happy.	Je suis content(e).
I'm sad.	Je suis triste.
I'm feeling better, thanks.	Ça va mieux, merci.

Greetings

Good morning.	Bonjour. Salut.
Good-bye.	Au revoir. Salut.
See you soon/tomorrow.	A bientôt/A demain.
Good night, sleep well.	Bonne nuit, dors bien.

Managing, activities

Can I have an ice cream, please?	Est-ce que je peux avoir une glace, s'il vous plaît?
Can I have your pen, please?	Je peux prendre ton stylo, s'il te plaît?
Thank you.	Merci.
What do you want?	Qu'est-ce que tu veux?
Pass me the pencil.	Passe-moi le crayon.
Where's the glue?	Où est la colle?

Where are the felt-tip pens? — Où sont les feutres?
It's on the table. — C'est sur la table.
Have you got the scissors? — As-tu les ciseaux?
Paste here. Cut there. — Colle-ici. Découpe-là.

Organizing games

Are you ready? Let's start. — Tu es prête? Commençons!
Let's play Lotto. — Jouons au Loto.
Go and get Lotto. — Va chercher le Loto.
You begin. — Tu commences.
It's your turn. — C'est à toi.
No. It's my turn. — Non. C'est à moi.
It's your turn again. — C'est encore à toi.
Well done. — Bien joué.
You've won. — Tu as gagné.
Put the cards here. — Mets les cartes ici.
Look. I've finished. — Voilà . J'ai fini.
I've lost the dice. — J'ai perdu le dé.
Deal the cards. — Donne les cartes.
Count to . . . — Compte jusqu'à . . .
You are red. I'm blue. (*counters*) — Toi, tu es rouge. Moi, je suis bleu.

Can I play, too? — Moi aussi, je peux jouer?
Go on quickly. — Allez-vite.
Show me . . . — Montre-moi.
Don't show your cards. — Ne montre pas tes cartes.
Take some. — Prends-en.
Don't take any. — N'en prends pas.

Language for understanding

What does that mean?	Qu'est-ce que ça veut dire?
I don't understand.	Je ne comprends pas.
How do you say *dog* in French?	Ça se dit comment *dog* en français?
How do you write it?	Ça s'écrit comment?
Say it again, please.	Répète-le, s'il te plaît.
How do you spell it?	Comment ça s'écrit?
Say the alphabet.	Récite l'alphabet.
Say the alphabet up to *g*.	Récite l'alphabet jusqu'á *g*.

Language for encouraging and praising

Bravo.	Bravo.
That's good.	Bien. C'est bien.
Try again. You can do it.	Essaie encore. Tu peux y arriver.
That's nice. I like that.	C'est joli. J'aime ça.

German

About me

I'm called . . .	Ich heiße . . .
I'm . . .	Ich bin . . .
I'm eight on . . .	Am . . .werde ich acht.
My birthday's on October 1st.	Ich habe am 1. Oktober Geburtstag.
I like playing soccer.	Ich spiele gerne Fußball.
I like watching television.	Ich sehe gerne fern.
I don't like swimming.	Ich schwimme nicht gerne.
Do you like cooking?	Kochst du gerne?
It's great.	Das ist toll.
I don't like it.	Das gefällt mir nicht.
I've got a watch.	Ich habe eine Uhr.
I'm wearing red socks today.	Heute habe ich rote Socken an.
My T-shirt is dirty.	Mein T-Shirt ist schmutzig.
Have you got a bag?	Hast du eine Tasche?
That's my book.	Das ist mein Buch.
Is that yours?	Gehört das dir?
I don't like chocolate.	Ich esse nicht gerne Schokolade.
Do you like ice cream?	Ißt du gerne Eis?
What's the matter?	Was ist denn los?
I feel sick.	Mir ist schlecht.
I've got a headache.	Mein Kopf tut weh.
I'm tired.	Ich bin müde.
I'm happy.	Ich bin glücklich.
I'm sad.	Ich bin traurig.
I'm feeling better, thanks.	Es geht mir besser, danke.

BEGINNING FRENCH, GERMAN, SPANISH, AND ITALIAN

Greetings

Good morning.	Guten Morgen.
Good-bye.	Auf Wiedersehen.
See you soon/tomorrow.	Bis bald/morgen.
Good night, sleep well.	Gute Nacht, schlaf gut.

Managing, activities

Can I have an ice cream, please?	Kann ich bitte ein Eis haben?
Can I have your pen, please?	Kann ich bitte deinen Bleistift haben?
Thank you.	Danke schön.
What do you want?	Was willst du?
Pass me the pencil.	Gib mir den Bleistift.
Where's the glue?	Wo ist der Kleber?
Where are the felt-tip pens?	Wo sind die Filzstifte?
It's on the table.	Er/sie/es ist auf dem Tisch.
Have you got the scissors?	Hast du die Schere?
Paste here. Cut there.	Klebe hier. Schneide dort.

Organizing/Games

Are you ready? Let's start.	Bist du fertig? Laß uns anfangen!
Let's play Lotto.	Laß uns Lotto spielen.
Go and get the Lotto.	Geh mal das Lotto holen.
You begin.	Du fängst an.
It's your turn.	Du bist dran.
No. It's my turn.	Nein. Ich bin dran.
It's your turn again.	Du bist wieder an der Reihe.
Well done.	Gut gemacht.
You've won.	Du hast gewonnen.
Put the cards here.	Leg die Karten hierher.
Look. I've finished.	Schau, ich bin fertig.
I've lost the dice.	Ich habe die Würfel verloren.

Deal the cards.	Gib die Karten aus.
Count to . . .	Zähl bis . . .
You are red. I'm blue. (*counters*)	Du hast rot.—Ich habe blau. (*Steine*)
Can I play too?	Kann ich auch mitspielen?
Go on quickly.	Beeil dich.
Show me . . .	Zeig mir . . .
Don't show your cards.	Halte deine Karten verdeckt.
Take some.	Ziehe ein paar (Karten).
Don't take any.	Ziehe keine (Karten).

Language for understanding

What does that mean?	Was bedeutet das?
I don't understand.	Ich verstehe nicht.
How do you say *dog* in German?	Wie sagt man *dog* auf Deutsch?
How do you write it?	Wie schreibt man das?
Say it again, please.	Sag das noch einmal, bitte.
How do you spell it?	Wie schreibt man das?
Say the alphabet.	Sag das Alphabet auf.
Say the alphabet up to *G*.	Sag das Alphabet bis *G* auf.

Language for encouraging and praising

Bravo.	Bravo.
That's good.	Das ist gut.
Try again. You can do it.	Versuch es noch einmal. Du kannst es.
That's nice. I like that.	Das ist schön. Das gefällt mir.

Spanish

About me

I'm called . . .
Me llamo . . .

I'm . . .
Soy . . .

I'm eight on . . .
Cumplo ocho anos . . . en

My birthday's on October 1st.
Mi cumpleanos es el primero de octubre.

I like playing soccer.
Me gusta jugar al fútbol.

I like watching television.
Me gusta mirar la television.

I don't like swimming.
No me gusta nadar.

Do you like cooking?
¿Te gusta cocinar?

It's great.
Es estupendo.

I don't like it.
No me gusta.

I've got a watch.
Tengo un reloj.

I'm wearing red socks today.
Hoy llevo calcetines rojos./ Tengo puestos calcetines rojos hoy.

My T-shirt is dirty.
Mi camiseta está sucia.

Have you got a bag?
¿Tienes una bolsa?

That's my book.
Ése es mi libro.

Is that yours?
¿Es tuyo eso?

I don't like chocolate.
No me gusta el chocolate.

Do you like ice cream?
¿Te gusta el helado?

What's the matter?
Qué pasa?

I feel sick.
Me siento enfermo.

I've got a headache.
Me duele la cabeza.

I'm tired.
Estoy cansado(a).

I'm happy.
Estoy contento(a)/feliz.

I'm sad.
Estoy triste.

I'm feeling better, thanks.
Me siento mejor, gracias.

Greetings

Good morning.	Buenos días.
Good-bye.	Adiós.
See you soon/tomorrow.	Hasta pronto./Hasta mañana.
Good night, sleep well.	Buenas noches. ¡ Que duermas bien!

Managing activities

Can I have an ice cream, please?	¿Puede darme un helado, por favor?
Can I have your pen, please?	¿Me dejas tu pluma, por favor?
Thank you.	Gracias.
What do you want?	¿Qué quieres?
Pass me the pencil.	Dame el lápiz. (*also:* Pásame el lápiz)
Where's the glue?	¿Dónde está el pegamento?
Where are the felt tip pens?	¿Dónde están los rotuladores?
It's on the table.	Está en la mesa.
Have you got the scissors?	¿Tienes las tijeras?
Paste here. Cut there.	Pega aquí. Corta allí.

Organizing/Games

Are you ready? Let's start.	¿Estás listo(a)?/Empecemos (vamos a empezar)
Let's play Lotto.	Juguemos a la Lotería.
Go and get Lotto.	Ve a comprar un billete de la Lotería.
You begin.	Tú empiezas.
It's your turn.	Te toca (a ti).
No. It's my turn.	No, me toca (a mí).
It's your turn again.	Te toca otra vez.
Well done.	Muy Bien.
You've won.	Has ganado.

BEGINNING FRENCH, GERMAN, SPANISH, AND ITALIAN

Put the cards here.	Pon las cartas aquí.
Look. I've finished.	Mira. He terminado.
I've lost the dice.	He perdido el dado.
Deal the cards.	Reparte las cartas. (*or:* Da las cartas.)
Count to . . .	Cuenta hasta . . .
You are red. I'm blue. (*counters*)	Tú eres la roja. Yo soy la azul. (*fichas*) (*las fichas*)
Can I play, too?	¿Puedo jugar yo también?
Go on quickly	Avanza rápidamente. (*or:* Avanza/Sigue, rápido).
Show me . . .	Enséñame . . .
Don't show your cards.	No enseñes tus cartas.
Take some.	Coge algunas.
Don't take any.	No cojas ninguna.

Language for understanding

What does that mean?	¿Qué significa eso?
I don't understand.	No comprendo.
How do you say *dog* in Spanish?	¿Cómo se dice *dog* en español?
How do you write it?	¿Cómo se escribe?
Say it again, please.	Repítelo, por favor.
How do you spell it?	¿Cómo se deletrea?/*or:* ¿Cómo se escribe?
Say the alphabet.	Di el abecedario (*or:* el alfabeto)
Say the alphabet up to *g*.	Di el abecedario (el alfabeto) hasta la *g*.

Language for encouraging and praising

Bravo	¡Bravo!
That's good.	Está muy bien.
Try again. You can do it.	Prueba otra vez. Puedes hacerlo.
That's nice. I like that.	Está muy bien. Me gusta eso.

Italian

About me

I'm called . . .	Mi chiamo . . .
I'm	Sono . . .
I'm eight on . . .	Compio otto anni il . . .
My birthday's on October 1st.	Il mio compleanno è il primo di ottobre.
I like playing football.	Mi piace giocare a calcio.
I like watching television.	Mi piace guardare la televisione.
I don't like swimming.	Non mi piace nuotare.
Do you like cooking?	Ti piace cucinare?
It's great.	È favoloso.
I don't like it.	Non mi piace.
I've got a watch.	Ho un orologio.
I'm wearing red socks today.	Oggi porto i calzini rossi.
My T-shirt is dirty.	La mia magliêtta è sporca.
Have you got a bag?	Hai un sacco?
That's my book.	Quello è il mio libro.
Is that yours?	Quello è tuo?
I don't like chocolate.	Il cioccolato non mi piace.
Do you like ice cream?	Ti piacciono i gelati?
What's the matter?	Che cosa c' è?
I feel sick.	Ho la nausea (I feel ill = Sto' male).
I've got a headache.	Ho mal di testa.
I'm tired.	Sona stanco (*feminine:* stanca).
I'm happy.	Sono felice.
I'm sad.	Sono triste.
I'm feeling better, thanks.	Sto meglio, grazie.

BEGINNING FRENCH, GERMAN, SPANISH, AND ITALIAN

Greetings

Good morning.	Buongiorno. Ciao.
Good-bye.	Arrivederci. Ciao. Buongiorno.
See you soon/tomorrow.	A presto/A domani.
Good night, sleep well.	Buonanotte, dormi bene.

Managing, activities

Can I have an ice cream please?	(*to mother*) Posso avere un gelato?
Can I have your pen, please?	Puoi prestarmi la penna?
Thank you.	Grazie.
What do you want?	Che cosa vuoi?
Pass me the pencil.	Passami la matita.
Where's the glue?	Dov'è la colla
Where are the felt-tip pens?	Dove sono i pennarelli?
It's on the table.	È sul tavolo.
Have you got the scissors?	Hai le forbici?
Paste here. Cut there.	Incolla qui. Taglia qui.

Organizing/Games

Are you ready? Let's start.	Sei pronto? (*masc.*)/Sei pronta? (*fem.*) Incominciamo
Let's play Lotto.	Giochiamo a tombola.
Go and get Lotto.	Vai a prendere la tombola.
You begin.	Comincia tu.
It's your turn.	Tocca a te.
No. It's my turn.	No, tocca a me.
It's your turn again.	Tocca di nuovo a te.
Well done.	Bene.
You've won.	Hai vinto.
Put the cards here.	Metti le carte qui.
Look, I've finished.	Guarda. Ho finito.
I've lost the dice.	Ho perso i dadi.

Deal the cards.	Distribuisci le carte.
Count to . . .	Conta fino a . . .
You are red. I'm blue. (*counters*)	Tu hai il rosso. Io ho il blu.
Can I play, too?	Posso giocare anch' io?
Hurry up.	Fa presto.
Show me . . .	Fammi vedere . . . (*or:* Mostrami . . .)
Don't show your cards.	Non far vedere (*or:* Non mostrare) le carte.
Take some.	Prendine un po'.
Don't take any.	Non prenderne.

Language for understanding

What does that mean?	Che cosa significa?
I don't understand.	Non capisco.
How do you say *dog* in Italian?	Come si dice *dog* in Italiano?
How do you write it?	Come si scrive?
Say it again, please.	Ripeti, per favore.
How do you spell it?	Come si scrive?
Say the alphabet.	Ripeti (*or:* Dimmi) l'alfabeto.
Say the alphabet up to *g*.	Ripeti (*or:* Dimmi) l'alfabeto fino alla *g*.

Language for encouraging and praising

Bravo.	Bravo. (*feminine:* Brava)
That's good.	Bene.
Try again. You can do it.	Prova ancora. Puoi riuscirci. (*or:* Puoi farcela)

Useful Addresses

Embassies and Consulates

French Embassy, 972 Fifth Avenue, New York, NY 10021

Italian Consulate, 690 Park Avenue, New York, NY 10021

German Consulate General, 460 Park Avenue, New York, NY 10022

Language Centers and Bookstores

For more information about Berlitz Publishing products, or to find the Berlitz Language Center nearest you, please call (800) 257-9449. In Canada, please call (800) 387-4776.

Berlitz Kids™ products can be found in your local bookstore, or at any of the following U.S. national retailers:

Barnes & Noble
Borders
Lauriat's
Learningsmith
Musicland
Noodle Kidoodle
Rizzoli Bookstores
Zany Brainy

In Canada:
Chapters

This is a sample of U.S. language and travel specialty booksellers. Please consult your yellow pages for additional information, or to locate a store in your area.

Book Passage, Corte Madera, CA
Books for Travel, St. Paul, MN
Complete Traveler, Overland Park, KS
Complete Traveller, New York, NY
Easy Going, Berkeley, CA
Globe Corner Bookstore, Boston, MA
Kinokuniya Bookstores (locations nationwide)
Latitudes, Atlanta, GA
Marco Polo, Seattle, WA
Phileas Fogg's Books & Maps, Palo Alto, CA
Powell's Travel Bookstore, Portland, OR
Rand McNally (locations nationwide)
Savvy Traveller, Chicago, IL
Schoenhof's Foreign Books, Cambridge, MA
Travel Books & Language Center, Washington, D.C.
Traveler's Emporium, Philadelphia, PA
Travelfest Superstores, Austin and Houston, TX
Voyages: The Travel Store, Dallas, TX

Index

NOTES

NOTES

NOTES

ABOUT BERLITZ

 In 1878 Professor Maximilian Berlitz had a revolutionary idea about making language learning accessible and enjoyable. One hundred and twenty years later these same principles are still successfully at work.

For language instruction, translation and interpretation services, cross-cultural training, study abroad programs, and an array of publishing products and additional services, visit any one of our more than 350 Berlitz Centers in 50 countries.

Please consult your local telephone directory for the Berlitz Center nearest you or visit our web site at http://www.berlitz.com.

Helping the World Communicate